Defending Diversity

Defending

Affirmative Action at th

PATRICIA GURIN,
JEFFREY S. LEHMAN,
AND EARL LEWIS

with
Eric L. Dey, Gerald Gurin,
and Sylvia Hurtado

Diversity
University of Michigan

Introduction by Nancy Cantor

Afterword by Mary Sue Coleman

UNIVERSITY OF MICHIGAN PRESS

ANN ARBOR

Copyright © by the University of Michigan 2004
All rights reserved
Published in the United States of America by
The University of Michigan Press
Manufactured in the United States of America
♾ Printed on acid-free paper

2007   2006   2005   2004   4   3   2   1

A CIP catalog record for this book is available from the British Library.

Library of Congress Cataloging-in-Publication Data

Defending diversity : affirmative action at the University of Michigan /
   Patricia Gurin . . . [et al.] ; introduction by Nancy Cantor / afterword
   by Mary Sue Coleman.
      p.   cm.
   Includes bibliographical references (p.   ) and index.
   ISBN 0-472-11307-0 (alk. paper)
      1. Universities and colleges—United States—Admission.   2. Minority
   college students—Recruiting—United States.   3. Affirmative action
   programs—United States.   4. Universities and colleges—Michigan—Ann
   Arbor—Admission.   5. Universities and colleges—Admission—Law and
   legislation—United States.   6. University of Michigan—Admission.   I.
   Gurin, Patricia.
   LB2351.2.D43   2004
   379.2'6'0973—dc22   2003026183

Contents

Introduction

Nancy Cantor

Good learning is always catholic and generous. It welcomes the humblest votary of science and bids him kindle his lamp freely at the common shrine. It frowns on caste and bigotry. It spurns the artificial distinctions of conventional society. It greets all comers whose intellectual gifts entitle them to admission to the goodly fellowship of cultivated minds. It is essentially democratic in the best sense of that term. . . . Let not a misapplication of the laissez-faire doctrine in political economy, which has its proper place, lead us to the fatal mistake of building up a pedantic aristocracy.

JAMES B. ANGELL,
president of the University of Michigan,
commencement address, June 25, 1879

One cannot sanction the desire for unity which seeks the complete fusion of individuals, racial strains, religious sections, social classes, national groups, or geographical areas—the elimination of their differences and the standardization of their character. . . . Under such circumstances, life would be impoverished; self-expression would be restrained; curiosity would be stifled; spontaneous experimentation would cease; the irrepressible yearning for progress would be repressed; conditions of status would displace the onward march of mind and hand and heart; the creative spark whereby men are moved to strive ever forward and upward would be dimmed if not extinguished; drab monotony would prevail. True unity is a matter of inward spirit rather than outward manifestation. It involves respect for differences rather than their elimination. . . . The road to such unity is understanding. The surest way to understanding is open-mindedness.

LEO SHARFMAN,
chair of the Department of Economics,
University of Michigan, speaking to Men's Club,
Temple Beth El, November 15, 1927

Universities rise in their places in the social landscape as affirmative expressions of our faith in the cumulative wisdom of the ages. . . . A university has a special responsibility for the guardianship of this heritage. But a university also has another responsibility. It must attempt to interpret the times in which it lives in order to meet the developing needs of the society which it serves. This means that it must be a comprehending observer of the present and, in so far as possible, a vehicle of understanding for the future. This is the great social mission of education in a free society. In the language of Disraeli, "A university should be a place of light, of liberty, and of learning."

JAMES P. ADAMS,
provost of the University of Michigan,
speech at the All-Class Dinner in commencement week,
June 15, 1950

My roommate and I roomed blind. I had no idea whom I would end up with. In mid-August I found out all about her. She was from Detroit and black. This didn't bother me one bit. So far we have gotten along great. . . . Here is one thing that I found funny. . . . My roommate has a flat iron that she uses to straighten AND curl her hair with. She had been bugging me for a while to let her try it on my hair. This one Friday night I decided to let her give it a try. . . . So she reached for my hair with her hand so that she could grab a chunk to brush. "Eeeee," she shrieked. "What is that?". . . . "No, nothing is wrong. I just can't believe what your hair feels like!". . . . "I've never felt any white girl's hair before," she said. "I had no idea it was so different." We spent the next hour discussing how we take care of our hair, how much it costs to get it done, and we also argued about what a perm is. This isn't a great educational story, but now I feel a little more "worldly" and not as sheltered as I had before. It's the little things like this that make impacts on my life. Small but nonetheless important. Diversity helps to make the world a little smaller.

UNIVERSITY OF MICHIGAN UNDERGRADUATE
responding in 1997 to an email request to all students from the
President of the Michigan Student Assembly to describe the
impact, positive or negative, of diversity in their life

The need to defend diversity came naturally and appropriately to the gates of the University of Michigan on October 14, 1997, when the papers for *Gratz v. Bollinger* were served, challenging affirmative action in undergraduate admissions. A second suit, *Grutter v. Bollinger,* was filed December 3, 1997, to challenge affirmative action in law school admissions.

It certainly was no coincidence that the Center for Individual Rights (CIR), the organization behind the lawsuits, chose as its target the University of Michigan, a great public research university, home to a long and storied history of political activism. Nestled near Detroit's Big Three factories in the middle of America, it also commanded the attention of its neighbors east and west. A victory at Michigan would certainly gain attention nationwide.

The CIR probably did not reckon fully either with the appropriateness or the consequences of suing the University of Michigan. The university's history has been extraordinarily rich in dialogues on diversity. Its distinguished alumni of all races, including former President Gerald Ford, stood ready to defend affirmative action and to bring to court the voices of America's corporate and military leadership. Michigan had much scholarly firepower, cultivated during more than fifty years of eminence in social science research, and diversity was ingrained as a primary value.

At any rate, the opponents of affirmative action did not take note of the University's historic commitments to diversity. James B. Angell, its third president, had entitled his 1879 commencement address "The Higher Education: A Plea for Making It Accessible to All." From its inception through the heyday of the Black Action Movement in the 1970s, the student newspaper, the *Michigan Daily,* had chronicled intergroup differences and conflicts. The campus had a deep familiarity with the subject. It had both expertise and hard-won tolerance. Michigan had a scholarly tradition of research on group dynamics that grew out of the anti-Semitism of the 1930s, 1940s, and 1950s. It was dedicated over many years to understanding intergroup relations, conflict, and community.

The opponents of affirmative action in admissions sorely underestimated the determination of the university, along with scores of peer institutions and professional societies, to defend its institutional mission. They also underestimated the fortitude of the students, scholars, alumni, and leaders they would confront. The plaintiffs in the case did not seem to realize that when General Motors spoke, the rest of corporate America would follow. To be truthful, it is fair to say that no one fully appreciated how a defense of diversity would resonate with corporate, military, and labor leaders or with members of the professions, who had come to see on a daily basis the need for—and benefits of—learning to live and work together. As Earl Lewis suggests in this volume, higher education—along with such training grounds as the military—is critical in this endeavor.

The Center for Individual Rights may also have underestimated the degree to which the nation's private universities would side with public universities in the struggle over affirmative action. Former presidents Derek Bok of Harvard and William G. Bowen of Princeton urged administrators and trustees, in their eloquent book *The Shape of the River,* to speak out loudly in its defense.

Scholars from Stanford's Center for Comparative Studies of Race and Ethnicity organized symposia as a call to action. Gary Orfield, Christopher Edley, Jr., and other members of Harvard's Civil Rights Project had documented the increasing segregation of the nation's high schools and brought into sharp focus the critical need to address the problem. Educational researchers at UCLA, Illinois, and Michigan could point to established national databases on the positive effects of integration.

As the many amicus briefs filed in the lawsuits showed, and as Justice O'Connor confirmed for the majority in *Grutter v. Bollinger,* the state has a weighty and compelling interest in making it possible for higher education to help write a positive story of race in America. Justice O'Connor wrote:

> The Law School's claim is further bolstered by numerous expert studies and reports showing that such diversity promotes learning outcomes and better prepares students for an increasingly diverse workforce, for society, and for the legal profession. Major American businesses have made clear that the skills needed in today's increasingly global marketplace can only be developed through exposure to widely diverse people, cultures, ideas, and viewpoints. High-ranking retired officers and civilian military leaders assert that a highly qualified, racially diverse officer corps is essential to national security. Moreover, because universities, and in particular, law schools represent the training ground for a large number of the Nation's leaders, *Sweatt v. Painter,* 339 U.S. 629, 634, the path to leadership must be visibly open to talented and qualified individuals of every race and ethnicity.[1]

As the essays in this book suggest, opponents of affirmative action failed to foresee how well the educational and societal purposes of diversity would fit within the pragmatic legal frameworks articulated by the Supreme Court in *Brown v. Board of Education* and in *Regents of the University of California v. Bakke.*

Fortunately, the Supreme Court revealed on June 23, 2003, that it had listened to America more closely than had the Center for Individual Rights.

A Special Place in Defending Diversity

In his commencement address in 1879, James B. Angell argued that the university had a special responsibility to cultivate the talents and abilities of all, no matter what their origin, to ensure that learning does not give way to pedantry "displayed like the ribbons and orders of a petty German court." It should also prepare to diffuse broadly across the land "men who are trained to be intelligent leaders of thought . . . to discharge the duties of citizenship." He made his plea for economic and social diversity "not merely on account of the poor and gifted scholars themselves, but also for the good of society."

Some 120 years later, his university structured its case for the compelling state interest of achieving diversity in higher education along strikingly similar lines.[2] The university documented persistent, though de facto, racial disparities in access to opportunity in virtually every aspect of American life, and took note of the entrenched patterns of segregation in housing, schooling, and employment. The university contended that higher education had a special role to play in engaging the potential for education and sharing its returns broadly. In doing so, it could stimulate critical thinking and creativity precisely because its students would encounter diversity unfamiliar to them. Such an education could prepare all kinds of future citizens to live and work across what President Angell in 1879 called "the artificial distinctions of conventional society."

The university's case for a compelling interest in diversity revolved around the special role that institutions of higher education must assume, as often the first and arguably the last opportunity for students to become citizens, soldiers, and workers comfortable in a racially and ethnically diverse America and inspired by it. Such an environment would improve learning and train better, more productive, more empathetic citizens and leaders.

This task was not to be assumed lightly. As scores of expert witnesses and hundreds of supporting amicus briefs reminded the Court, race still matters in profound ways in American society. Race still delineates the haves and the have-nots. Racial stereotypes and conflict undermine our productivity, security, and the harmony of our democracy. The words of the witnesses in these cases were resonant, and therefore haunting, echoes of those spoken by Governor Otto Kerner some thirty years earlier, as he summarized the results of his commission's investigation of race riots in over 150 American cities in one summer.

Our nation is moving toward two societies, one black, one white—separate and unequal. Discrimination and segregation have long permeated much of American life; they now threaten the future of every American.[3]

For race to stop mattering in destructive ways and start mattering in productive ways, we had to keep trying what President Angell had advocated way back in 1879. Of course we couldn't, nor could he, "take all comers." But universities had to start making choices where few had been made before. We had to include more of America's talent, training leaders who would carry their education "out into the land."

For this country to move together peacefully, it would not suffice to integrate the boot camps and not the military academies, the juror boxes and not the judiciary, the emergency room and not the operating theater, the factory and not the boardroom, the classroom and not the professoriate, the voting booth and not the Congress. Real integration cannot happen until Americans of all colors learn with and from each other in the best classrooms of this land.

Learning Together

Learning is hard work, best done in the company of others. The educational benefits of diversity, as any honest educator must acknowledge, come largely from the social infrastructure of the "classroom." This is what Leo Sharfman knew in 1927 and what the Michigan roommates knew as they worked on their hair in 1997. It is also what lay at the heart of the two Supreme Court decisions that served as precedent in the Michigan cases.

[Separating black schoolchildren] from others of similar age and qualifications solely because of their race generates a feeling of inferiority as to their status in the community that may affect their hearts and minds in a way unlikely ever to be undone.

CHIEF JUSTICE WARREN,
1954, *Brown v. Board of Education*

It is not too much to say that the "nation's future depends upon leaders trained through wide exposure" to the ideas and mores of students as diverse as this nation of many peoples.

JUSTICE POWELL
in *Regents of the University of California v. Bakke*,
citing Justice Brennan's opinion in writing for the majority in
1967 in *Keyishian v. Board of Regents*

Brown and *Bakke* both drew on findings from social science, and both decisions saw intelligence and excellence from a fundamentally *social* perspective: that is, education and learning are socially shared activities that depend in large part on the quality and effectiveness of the mix of people and ideas in the environment.

The social science data used in these cases, as spearheaded by Gurin et al. in her expert testimony in both cases in the U.S. District Court and summarized in this volume, significantly extend

our understanding of just how *social* learning turns out to be. The quality of thinking, its vibrancy, and its resonance depend on whether the learner is challenged in his or her social environment—whether the ideas and voices in formal classes or in everyday campus life sound different enough to add discipline to our normal "mindless" habits. A new idea, a different way of saying the same thing, a question from left field; all enrich the learning environment.

Here, disequilibrium matters. It encourages us to pay attention, to see ourselves and the world in a slightly new light. To achieve this social disequilibrium, in which peers shed that new light, it helps to have diversity, in which the person in the next seat may well ask a question from a different perspective. That variation, in turn, will challenge others to notice and to think.

Why does race matter in this disequilibrium equation? It matters because, whether by design early in our history or through our failure to discard the legacy of Jim Crow, we are still largely segregated by race and ethnicity in our daily lives.[4] It is those experiences, embedded in the rituals of living—in how we fix our hair, how we celebrate our birthdays and mourn at our funerals—that lay the groundwork for the rich tapestry of perspectives brought to the table when a diverse student body learns together. Race becomes a metaphor for crossing the sensibilities of alternative life experiences. Race is not the only metaphor, but it is an important one, historically and in our own times.

In maximizing the likelihood of students experiencing perspectives, voices, ideas, and passions, is race all that matters? Of course not. In 1879, President Angell made the same argument in favor of the different perspectives brought from different regions of the country and different socioeconomic sectors of society. Sharfman made it for religion in 1927. Ira Smith, Michigan's registrar from 1925 to 1955, made it to defend the vigorous recruitment and support of veterans under the G.I. Bill. But while race and ethnicity are not the only sources of difference, it is also true that students of color and white students from all walks of American life have experienced the world in such different ways that getting them together offers a rich range of educational possibilities that their heretofore separate lives have obscured from view.

Of course, creating the social conditions for the kind of expansive learning experiences we desire will not be easy, in view of the pervasiveness of stereotypes that threaten individuals' performance, as testified to by Claude Steele in his expert testimony in the lawsuits.[5] But we can never hope to fully engage the talents of all Americans unless we try to build on what Steele refers to as "wise" learning environments—and these must be significantly welcoming and inclusive of our nation's multiracial and ethnically diverse population.

Living Together

The social learning that can follow from a diverse student body goes even further than promoting cognitive challenges and stellar performances. We must help construct environments for intergroup relations that pave the way for racial integration—for living and working harmoniously together across the lines of race in America. This is an endeavor that takes hard work, including a willingness not to paper over discomfort, mistrust, fear, or even conflict. There is bound to be a wariness on all sides that comes both from the absence of experience with integration and from concerns about social identity. As Sharfman eloquently stated in his descriptions of intergroup relations and religious tensions on campus in 1927, for "unity" to be positive, it must engage genuine difference. This requires many individual acts of will, encouraged by a learning environment that places a premium on getting to know each other.

We all have a long way to go in getting to know each other, as the following excerpt from expert testimony in the Michigan cases suggests:

> Most Michigan residents live in neighborhoods that are not diverse racially or ethnically. . . . Blacks and whites seldom talk across the fence. They rarely meet casually on the streets. . . . They do not attend each other's birthday parties or belong to the same social clubs and churches or attend town meetings together. . . . As teenagers, they rarely hang out together in malls or go on camping trips together or date. . . . Chance events or rituals, profound moments of bonding, or everyday social interactions—these are the fabric of everyday life, the basis of relationships, of community, of commonality. Whites and non-whites are usually not part of each other's daily routines or witness to each other's life-changing events.[6]

But at their best, universities can be safe havens for the development of just such a community, based on intergroup dialogue, the civil airing of conflict among students who, as peers, perceive each other as equals. This develops a capacity for participating in democracy, for integration, and for social harmony. No one thinks this happens easily or automatically—after all, most of these students, like most of us, have precious little experience airing differences in integrated settings, and both students of color and white students naturally would prefer the ease and comfort afforded by familiarity and similarity. But it does happen, and even one or two such experiences can set a course for life, as Gurin et al. demonstrated in their expert report.[7]

The Michigan Student Study, as Gurin notes in this volume, repeatedly heard from students about this interweaving of experiences of conflict and of community as they navigated, often for the first time, a diverse living and learning environment. How could it be otherwise, with so little prior practice? Students, majority and minority, report experiencing racial tension and discord on campus at the very same time they report having made one or more close friends, often for the first time, of another race/ethnicity. In fact, as seniors, 91 percent of white students, 94 percent of Asian American students, 79 percent of African American students, and 87 percent of Latino students in the study agreed that "my relationships with students of different ethnic/racial groups have been positive."

These experiences set the stage for replacing unfair stereotypes, even the favorable ones, with something more individual and realistic. An exposure to group similarities and differences may well give students a more perceptive assessment of the variations they find within their own groups, as well as respect for students from different cultural, racial, or ethnic backgrounds. All of this tends to make the world "a little smaller," as the anonymous student reported on the basis of doing her hair with her roommate.

Defending Affirmative Action

Our need to consider the nation's compelling interest in affirmative action turned our attention squarely to its benefits, which include drawing on a full talent pool in ways that broaden the opportunities for social/economic mobility for more Americans. By bringing a more diverse group of students to campus, we are in the position to educate all students in an environment where they will be challenged to see new possibilities for themselves and their world because of the mix of voices and perspectives at the table. Hardest of all, but most significantly, these experiences will, as they become more numerous, ultimately prepare all students to live and work in harmony in a multiracial democracy.

Side by side with this story of the nation's compelling interest in diversity runs a more negative story, anchored in the troubled history of race in America, in which race has been used as a weapon of discrimination against individuals. The Court addressed this story in *Brown,* in which it ruled that, under the Fourteenth Amend-

ment, children of color must be protected from the pernicious consequences of separate, and therefore, unequal treatment at the hands of institutions that hold the keys to the gates of opportunity. It is this second story that makes us leery of the direct consideration of race, as Lehman articulates in this volume, even as we know that we must directly confront race, and do so in ways that uncloak our prejudices and ignorance.

It is also the story behind the "strict scrutiny" test for race-conscious procedures, a test given form in Justice Powell's narrow tailoring in *Bakke* of a "plus-factor" approach that minimizes the burden on majority applicants. Such an approach manages at once to be race-conscious but not overly explicit in its use of race as a factor, allowing race to be one factor among many in the individualized evaluation of all applicants.

Such an individualized evaluation assures that all who are admitted to the university will be qualified and prepared to succeed, avoiding the possibility of a cynical trade-off between diversity and excellence. No rigid quota, no separate and unequal process, may be employed. Nothing overly mechanistic may be employed. Therefore, there is no temptation to "overweight" race, perhaps by automatically assigning set numbers of points to everyone who fits a label, a practice the Court struck down in *Gratz v. Bollinger*. This is the flexible and largely subjective approach endorsed by Michigan's law school in 1992 and supported by the majority of the Court in *Grutter v. Bollinger*.

Opponents of affirmative action may have underestimated just how reasonable the public would find this pragmatic compromise. Listen to the editorializing from the *Arizona Republic*, written before Justice O'Connor, herself an Arizonian, wrote her historic opinion in *Grutter*.

We believe that there is a compelling educational interest in ensuring diversity and that using race as one factor, not the only factor, not the single most important factor, is a legally acceptable and socially responsible action in a country less than 40 years removed from poll taxes and literacy tests.[8]

Why was this approach so compelling? This version of "plus-factor" affirmative action satisfies both the legalists' desire for subtlety when it comes to race, and the social scientists' desire to bring a critical mass of well-qualified students of color prepared to succeed in selective institutions across our country.

Moreover, as scholars in the Harvard Civil Rights Project persuasively argued, there really are no effective alternative systems that achieve the goals of race-conscious policies.[9] Percentage plans, in which the top 4, 10, or 20 percent, say, of any state high school is guaranteed a place at the state university, narrow the evaluation process to one quite imperfect measure, class rank, without an eye toward preparation. They only succeed if neighborhoods continue to be as segregated as they have been. Plans that rely solely on giving weight to socioeconomic disadvantage fail to provide for a racially diverse student body at selective institutions[10] and give no attention to recruiting a critical mass of students of color with experiences from all walks of life.

But even more importantly, many Americans are committed to writing a positive story of race. They know it is critically important to pay direct attention to race so we can move beyond our history. As the social psychologists in the Michigan cases testified, we as a nation will find it very difficult, if not impossible, to counter the pernicious and automatic activation of stereotypes and intergroup fears—and the prejudice and discrimination that follow—unless we can talk directly and persistently about race. Proxies are not useful in this highly charged and contested arena.[11]

The significance of the arguments about "critical mass" made in the Michigan cases is underscored by decades of social science research that shows the ameliorative effects of intergroup contact, especially when each group is itself represented by individuals with a wide range of life experiences.[12]

Many people believe that a necessary step—and a positive one—in moving beyond our troubled history is to do what we always do in admissions: to make choices between qualified students and to use scarce resources affirmatively with race and ethnicity in mind.

In fact, as Peter Irons suggests in his stunning volume *Jim Crow's Children: The Broken Promise of the Brown Decision*,[13] there is legal precedent for this view in the opinions of Judge John Minor Wisdom in his 1966 opinion in *United States v. Jefferson County Board of Education*, and in Justice Harry Blackmun's concurring opinion in *Bakke* twelve years later.

> The Constitution is both color blind and color conscious. To avoid conflict with the Equal Protection clause, a classification that denies a benefit, causes harm, or imposes a burden must not be based on race. In that sense, the Constitution is color blind. But the Constitution is color conscious to prevent discrimination being perpetuated and to undo the effects of past discrimination. The criterion is the relevance of color to a legitimate governmental purpose. (Judge John Minor Wisdom, 1966)[14]

> In order to get beyond racism, we must first take account of race. There is no other way. (Justice Harry Blackmun, 1978)[15]

As supporters of affirmative action have argued, it is time for educators to lay their values out directly, to rewrite the American imagination about race. One way to begin is to send a powerful message in college and university admissions that we, as educators, *affirmatively value* the contributions of students of color and are therefore willing to use such scarce resources as the seats in our classes because we want them at the table.

We must get to know each other if we are to profit individually and collectively from our diverse talents. As those writing an amicus brief on behalf of the AFL-CIO suggested, "higher education represents a unique opportunity and, from the vantage point of the workplace, the last opportunity, to foster interaction between diverse individuals."[16]

That, more than anything, is what defending diversity in higher education is about. That, fortunately, is what the Supreme Court affirmed on June 23, 2003. This affirmation is a victory for America, raising our hopes that we can move from a troubled history to an integrated future.

Affirmative action alone won't create that new future. Integration is hard work—harder than rocket science, to paraphrase Christopher Edley, Jr. Now is the time to redouble our efforts.

Why History Remains a Factor in the Search for Racial Equality

Earl Lewis

The conversation began innocently enough. "So how do you think of yourself?" we asked. A light-skinned child of six, the product of an interracial marriage, she without hesitation responded, "I am black, African American." "Why?" came the question from both parents' mouths even before we realized the consequences or implications of what we had just asked. With a tone that suggested surprise at our need to ask, she pronounced, "If slavery still existed, I would be a slave." The young girl whose sense of self could not be erased from the history of race in America was my six-year-old daughter Suzanne. Even at that tender age she knew enough about her country to comprehend that she could not live outside of history and its meanings in everyday interactions. As a nation and society we had created race, and she was a by-product of that history; in and out of school she had been so educated. Unwittingly, she joined a long list of scholars in saying that race was an historically manufactured social construction and had a lingering effect on all. No matter how much she might have desired, she could not escape that history.

This essay does more than retrace that history; it explores the link between past events and contemporary public policy. It begins with a review of the constitutional debates over access to education, especially higher education, culminating in the landmark 1978 *Bakke* decision. It briefly reviews the imperatives for adopting affirmative action policies in the United States during the late 1960s and the early 1970s. It argues that federal officials responded to real disparities in life choices and material conditions and that the policies adopted were rooted in the history of racial discrimination in the United States. To underscore this point, I rely almost exclusively on black-white comparisons, while acknowledging that affirmative action benefited American Indians, Latinos and Latinas, Asian Americans in some instances, and white women. Rather than examine all sectors of society, the second half of the essay looks closely at diversity in higher education. I conclude with two essential points. First, policies designed to insure equitable access to opportunity produce a more civic-minded citizenry, which was a key reason for the introduction of affirmative action. Second, the introduction of affirmative action cannot and should not be divorced from the particulars of a given society. In the American context, this meant that action by public and private institutions intended to both correct past inequities and produce societal gains. With the latter in mind, those same policymakers sought to take advantage of the diverse talents and skills that deserved to be nurtured, assuming that in doing so they served the larger goal of furthering the aims of the democratic society. That the debate over affirmative action roils one nation reflects the United States' continued encounter with its racial dilemma. That ethnic hostilities have surfaced in a number of world settings reminds us of the problem difference plays in all societies. Failure to acknowledge and address the dilemmas of ethnic integration could prove a vexing and enduring problem for the world in the twenty-first century.

The Continued Encounter with the American Dilemma

Nearly six decades ago Gunnar Myrdal, aided by the prodigious research skills of a team of social scientists, forced an intellectual and philosophical confrontation: He and his colleagues exposed the profound differences between the American ideal and the American reality. As a liberal democracy, the United States had long been hailed as a "shining city on a hill," an example of the best in human potential, where, some claimed, caste, class, religion, gender, and race were social markers but not barriers to success and achievement. From the foothills of Appalachia through the dense thicket of ethnic urban enclaves, across the barren landscapes of the West, another narrative competed. It described an America where social markers limited the height of one's accomplishments and narrowed the scope of one's dreams. Myrdal's effort to understand those two Americas culminated in the publication of *An American Dilemma*, which he subtitled *The Negro Problem and Modern Democracy*.[1]

Race, Myrdal concluded after his research, played a significant role in America. That the study commenced during the Great Depression, when black unemployment rose substantially, underscored rather than distorted what minority status meant in a democratic society. From our vantage point of the early twenty-first century rather than the midpoint of the twentieth, one might contest the juxtaposition of *Negro* and *problem*. After all, the special place of African Americans in the country's life and history had as much to do with others as it did with the descendants of the enslaved Africans who labored so mightily in the fields, farms, and factories before the Civil War. Yet in looking at a modern democracy that denied its full benefits to a subordinated, racialized population, Myrdal identified a disjunction that still vexes the United States and the scholars who study the ways of its citizenry.

The American Negro problem is a problem in the heart of the American. It is there that interracial tension has its focus. It is there that the decisive struggle goes on. The "American Dilemma," referred to in the title of this book, is the ever-raging conflict between . . . the valuation preserved on the general plane which we shall call the "American Creed," . . . and . . . the valuations on specific planes of individual and group living.[2]

Using the vernacular of the last century's first years, which celebrated a general support for democracy and freedom for all Americans, Myrdal asked how to achieve a just society without violating the perceptions of justice and fairness, especially if laws were introduced to protect or advance the interests of a few. How does one realize equity in a society when the focus is often on equality, especially when equity represents the process of becoming equal?[3]

In the half century and more since Myrdal compiled his observations, much has changed in America. The most rigid, state-enforced examples of racial discrimination live only in the memories of those old enough to have experienced the bitter sting or sweet benefits of legal segregation. Americans are today free to pursue affairs of the heart across the color line without governmental interference or opposition, free to live where their finances permit, open to attend schools and colleges of their choice and means based on factors other than just the color of their skin. Income disparities have narrowed, educational attainment levels have converged for select portions of the general population, and life expectancy, to name a few examples, no longer diverge as markedly.

Yet the tension Myrdal so brilliantly pinpointed remains a source of civic injury. Racial difference and intolerance can inflame as openly today as in the past. Hardly a day goes by when some example of the capacity to hate, often in a murderous fashion, outshines examples of tolerance. For commentators such as Dinesh D'Souza, who insist that racism is a feature of the past and not the future,[4] come reminders that it is impossible for most of us to completely step outside of history. In popular culture, academic treatises, social analyses, advice on marriage mates, and families squabbles about friends, we are reminded that race, and our unavoidably incomplete analysis of it, figures significantly in the state policies adopted.

Deep Roots

America's encounter with the dilemma of race began the day nineteen Africans entered colonial Jamestown and became bonded labor. More than two centuries of slavery, a Civil War, and periods of reconstruction and redemption added new chapters but did not alter the main storyline: race marked blacks as second class in American life. By the end of the nineteenth century the spring of hope that followed the abolition of slavery gave way to the winter of despair, or what historian Rayford Logan called the nadir. Extralegal violence, political disfranchisement, and growing residential segregation increased across the South and much of America.[5]

A way of life evolved for blacks, whites, and others. In the South, racial groups lived in both the bright light and the shadows of one another's existence. On one level work patterns meant that blacks often had intimate knowledge of the folkways, thoughts, and behavior of whites. As in slavery, they saw whites for whom they worked at their best and worst. On another level, perceptions of supremacy meant that few whites saw most blacks as intimate equals, for they were not. Laws and local ordinances appeared that regulated human interaction. The system under which all lived became known as Jim Crow, or segregation. At its most basic level the system separated blacks from whites in things sublimely routine and in matters perversely significant—birth registers, water fountains, cemeteries, and telephone directories, for example.

The period from the 1890s to 1940 was more than a tragic story in American race relations; it was a period characterized by pronounced violence. Lynchings, mass murders, convict labor, debt peonage, abject poverty, and more subtle but nonetheless pernicious forms of racism shaped black and white lives for nearly three generations. In this contrived world the lowliest white assumed domain over the most successful black. Looking back from the twenty-first century, some may find it convenient to dismiss this ugly period in American history or to inflate the power of white authority. Many blacks managed for days and weeks at a time to live beyond the stare of white eyes. That too was a central dimension of Jim Crow life. They saw themselves as more than victims; they were full men, women, and children trying to chart lives in a sometimes inhospitable world. Yet victimization was not a figment but a real possibility, one that all blacks feared and one that elders explained to their charges so they could avoid death.[6]

At the local and national levels blacks organized to thwart the system of segregation. They created national protest organizations, used political contacts and involvement to champion their own interests, and engineered efforts to challenge the legality of Jim Crow legislation.[7] Throughout the history of struggle against the system, the courts of the land played a profoundly central role, especially the U. S. Supreme Court.

In the 1890s the battle lines of the fight for justice and opportunity centered on the Deep South. New Orleans had been a cultural and racial crossroads; there the different strands of Europe knotted with the ethnic fibers of Africa to produce a creole tapestry seldom found in the continental United States. In a tripartite arrangement, African, Europeans, and their progeny claimed their distinct places on the quilt of social relations that distinguished New Orleans, notwithstanding the existence of slavery, from other southern places.[8]

In New Orleans Homer Adolph Plessy joined a group of others incensed by new limits imposed on them on public conveyances. Many blacks feared, and a number of whites hoped, that a new racial covenant was soon to emerge, one that established the sanctity of segregation. Plessy, seven-eighths white but nonetheless black according to state law, believed that the 1890 Louisiana law, the Act to Promote the Comfort of Passengers, violated his rights. The law specified that "all railway companies carrying passengers in their coaches in this State, shall provide equal but separate accommodations for the white, and colored races, by providing two or more passenger coaches for each passenger train, or by dividing the passenger coaches by a partition so as to secure separate accommodations."⁹ Railway executives frowned on the provision as unnecessary and an additional financial burden. For nearly two years train workers all but ignored the prohibitions, allowing blacks to sit according to arrival and class of ticket, although companies did add cars for "coloreds only." Upset by the law and what it implied, blacks pushed to have the law abolished.

On June 7, 1892, a coordinated challenge took place. That day Plessy claimed his seat on the East Louisiana Railway as the train journeyed thirty miles north of New Orleans, headed to Covington. Through a prearranged signal, Plessy moved to the section reserved for whites, only to immediately be asked to return to his seat. Given Plessy's appearance, it is highly unlikely that the conductor could discern race from a quick glance. That a detective stood ready to arrest him when he refused to surrender his seat suggests a coordinated action. Soon Plessy found himself before a magistrate in New Orleans, who found that he had knowingly and willfully violated the state ordinance. Plessy appealed the ruling to the Louisiana Supreme Court, which allowed him to take his case directly to the U.S. Supreme Court.

Four years after the initial act of civil disobedience, the Supreme Court issued its decision. Henry Billings Brown wrote the majority opinion, which codified the legal principle of separate but equal. The court's majority concluded that as long as blacks had nominally equal access to resources, the state could devise strategies to separate them from whites. The constitution, the majority reasoned, could not place blacks and whites on the same social plane.¹⁰

Over the course of the next two generations the critical issue would become what constituted equal opportunity.

Within twelve years of the 1896 *Plessy* decision the Supreme Court ventured into the territory of higher education. Berea College in Kentucky, a private institution, had been tied to an interracialist sentiment since its 1859 founding. School officials believed that the welfare of the nation turned on the ability to educate a leadership, guided by Christian principles, that could work with other groups. The school had been founded as a place where blacks and whites would encounter one another as relative equals (prohibitions against interracial dating notwithstanding). Opposed to the commingling, the state of Kentucky inserted itself. The state introduced legislation that required school officials to teach blacks and whites at separate times in separate locations. This set in motion a legal fight that ultimately landed in Washington, D.C.[11]

The Supreme Court upheld the legality of the Kentucky legislation, arguing that the state of Kentucky could regulate human interaction at public as well as private institutions because the state had authorized the incorporation of the school. The constitutional prerogative did little to hide the net effect: segregation provisions drew invidious distinctions between whites and blacks. The language was highly visible in the Kentucky statute:

> If the progress, advancement and civilization of the twentieth century is to go forward, then it must be left, not only to the unadulterated blood of the Anglo-Saxon-Caucasian race, but to the higher types and geniuses of that race.[12]

In fact, *Berea College v. Kentucky* accented the understood logic: segregation was not devised to benefit blacks but rather to insure that the interests of whites prevailed.

It did not take two generations before African Americans and their friends began to fight back. Even during the formative years of segregation individual blacks managed to attend the most selective colleges and universities. Private schools such as Amherst, Brown, and Harvard, and public universities such as Minnesota, Michigan, and UCLA counted a black graduate or two among their alums in the 1910s and 1920s. From this small cadre emerged a growing black intelligentsia, which included the legal theorists and strategists William H. Hastie and Charles Howard Houston, and such towering figures as Alain Locke, E. Franklin Frazier, and Ralph Bunche. From their seats at Howard University they came to train among others the future Supreme Court justice Thurgood Marshall.[13]

Marshall had been raised in Baltimore, Maryland, a state on the figurative middle ground between slave and free. After the abolition of slavery and the institutionalization of Jim Crow, the state had begun to behave more southern, providing "separate but equal" educational opportunities and accommodations for blacks and whites. Notably absent in the state during the 1930s was a law school for blacks. Marshall knew this firsthand. He had aspired to attend the University of Maryland Law School after graduating from Lincoln University in Pennsylvania, but it had no place for blacks. This was true when he, Houston, and local NAACP officials agreed to challenge the legality and propriety of segregation.[14]

A case that appeared in legal annals as *Murray v. Pearson* but many contemporaries considered *Murray v. Maryland* was the first victory in the fight for equal opportunity in higher education. Donald Murray had applied to attend the law school at the University of Maryland only to be told the school did not admit blacks. University president Raymond Pearson explained in a letter to Murray that the state legislature had earmarked funds for him to attend law school out of state or at Morgan State or Princess Anne Academy. The latter, hardly an institution of higher education, highlighted the artifice of segregation's claim of separate but equal facilities and institutions. At best a high school, neither it, nor Morgan State, offered law degrees. In a 1935 exchange of letters with the registrar and the president of the University of Maryland, Murray wrote, "I am a citizen of the State of Maryland and fully qualified to become a student at the University of Maryland Law School. No other State institution affords a legal education."

Houston's opening comments to the Baltimore City Court that heard the case were framed by Murray's aims and assessment of his own skills and desires, and by the university's actions. State university officials became unwitting assistants for the NAACP lawyers. They willingly offered that there was no law school for blacks in the state; showed little sense that one should exist, even a patently unequal one; admitted that the state had not appropriated funds to send Murray out of state; and evinced little concern for even the crudest elements of the *Plessy* doctrine. At the conclusion of the hearing Judge Eugene O'Dunne ordered the university to admit Murray to the University of Maryland Law School. Appeals followed but to no avail. Murray had made his case and won.[15]

What Maryland judges decided had little reach beyond the state's borders. NAACP lawyers and those they defended understood this. Incremental change brought little relief for the majority of blacks seeking a fair share of resources. Yet the body of law rested on the establishment of precedent. Thus a gradualist approach continued.

Meanwhile, potential plaintiffs and strategists set their sights on another border state, Missouri. There were few black lawyers in the state, even in its largest city, St. Louis. As in Maryland, no law school existed for blacks, and they could not attend the law school at the exclusively white state public university. As in Maryland, blacks had the option of attending one of the state-sanctioned black institutions, where a law program would be created, or of attending a law school out of state. If a black resident of Missouri opted for the latter, the state would pay the difference in tuition between Missouri costs and that school's costs. The state had no allowances for travel or accommodations, however.

Lloyd Gaines, a graduate of all-black Lincoln University of Missouri, sought admission to the University of Missouri's law school. He rejected the state's legitimate offer to build a law program at Lincoln or to travel out of state, saying that doing so would place an undue burden on him and deny him equal rights just because of his race. Charles Houston argued this point before the Missouri state courts in 1936 in *Missouri ex. rel Gaines v. Canada*. Missouri officials took few risks. They assembled a team of skilled attorneys and provided evidence of a willingness to maintain separate yet quality institutions for blacks. After weighing the arguments, the state court rejected Gaines's complaint.

Within two years the case made its way to the U.S. Supreme Court. Against the backdrop of the depression and agitation for social inclusion and improvement from a broad swath of Americans, the Court's traditional role as a conservative protector of the interests of a few began to change. By the second half of the 1930s the Court questioned the constitutionality of all-white juries, validated the right of workers to engage in collective bargaining, and rethought the state's role in the policing of individual debt, among other things. It was this Court that heard Houston's appeal on behalf of Gaines and agreed with his logic that the remedies suggested by the state of Missouri placed undue burden on Gaines. Houston did not attack the logic of segregation in Gaines; instead, he extended that logic, suggesting that minus the immediate construction of a first-rate law school for blacks, the State of Missouri violated its promise of separate but equal opportunities for all. Rather than a frontal attack on segregation, which had the greatest likelihood of ameliorating persecution, lynching, poverty, and the heavy cross of racism, Houston played another game: if black people must be treated differently and poorly, then do so justly as outlined by the law. The majority accepted this argument, writing,

The basic consideration is not to what sort of opportunities other states provide, or whether they are as good as those of Missouri, but as to what opportunities Missouri itself furnishes to white students and denies to Negroes solely upon the ground of color. The admissibility of laws separating the races in the enjoyment of privileges afforded the State rests wholly upon the equality of the privileges which the laws give to the separated groups within the State. . . . By the operation of the laws of Missouri a privilege has been created for the white law students which is denied to Negroes by reason of their race.[16]

Thus through the 1930s the logic of segregation went unassailed in the legal arena. Since the 1920s black social scientists had been writing that race was a social construction. African American novelists penned a number of works of fiction throughout the 1920s and 1930s questioning the legitimacy and efficacy of segregation for both blacks and whites. Yet racial difference mattered as much as ever as the nation entered into World War II. Where change had occurred, it entailed accepting European immigrants as other than distinct and separate races. Increasingly over the first four decades of the twentieth century a new understanding took hold. Hostile speculations about the racial pedigree of eastern and southern Europeans slowly evaporated. Without exception, all with European ancestry became white. And where questions remained, they became household questions rather than public policy pronouncements acted on by politicians, newspaper moguls, and other shapers of public opinion and policy. Every significant social relationship, from whom one could marry to where one could live to which colleges one could attend, reflected this change, which World War II hastened.[17]

For Japanese Americans the war underscored their difference and the primacy of race. Unlike Italian and German Americans, their ancestry, appearance, and race marked them as dangerous and thus a threat to national security. In response California governor Earl Warren had them detained; their property was confiscated and their lives uprooted. Before the war's end, Japanese Americans, irrespective of place of birth, found themselves relocated to isolated hamlets across the West. Called internment camps rather than concentration camps, the barbed wire enclosures served some of the same purposes, although they did not lead to the same deadly consequences.[18]

The war did not produce a fundamental change in life circumstances for African Americans. Segregation remained a staple of American life. Black G.I.s, often in uniform, endured the biting sting of Jim Crow. Across the South white-owned establishments directed black soldiers to the back for service, even when dressed in the colors of the armed services. They trained and served in segregated units; they were assigned to menial, sometimes extremely hazardous duties, such as loading and unloading armaments. When they challenged the status quo, they ran afoul of military protocol and became subjects of court martial. Nonetheless, at home and abroad African Americans used the war to demonstrate their patriotism and to agitate for change.[19]

The war's end brought a new wave of legal challenges from African Americans seeking access to higher education. More than other border states, Oklahoma vigorously worked to separate blacks and whites in educational settings at all levels, going so far as to impose fines on those willing to foster interracial instruction. In 1946 a highly accomplished, spirited, though shy graduate of Langston College for Negroes, Ada Sipuel, applied for admission to the University of Oklahoma Law School, which denied her application. Thurgood Marshall, who by now had taken over as general legal counsel for the NAACP, thought Sipuel's situation bore a striking similarity to the *Murray* and *Gaines* cases. In the intervening years, however, Marshall's view on segregation had evolved. For the first time, Marshall expressed doubt that a society committed to equality could effect that equality through segregation. Cautiously, he was prepared to expose "separate but equal" as a social and constitutional fraud.

The Regents of the University of Oklahoma would have nothing to do with such an argument. Heading to trial, they pronounced that they were prepared to build a separate law school for blacks. The full logic of this position only became clear in court when lawyers for the state realized that building separate facilities for blacks in all areas would amount to a staggering expense. The economics of segregation notwithstanding, the lower court upheld the position of the state. On appeal the state again prevailed.

In 1948 the U.S. Supreme Court heard *Sipuel.* With quick dispatch the Court ruled that Oklahoma had to build an equal law school for blacks, admit Sipuel to the present law school, or close it altogether until blacks could be accommodated. Once the case was remanded to the state courts for enforcement, the board of regents reacted with open disdain. They brazenly roped off a section of the state capital for the special instruction of Ada Sipuel. Marshall found this a wanton act of discrimination and again appealed to the Supreme Court. This time he inched closer to assaulting the whole edifice of segregation, suggesting that equality hinged on free exchange of ideas and interactions, which segregation could never produce. In this appeal Marshall distanced himself from the logic of separate but equal. He, unfortunately, was ahead of the Court, which sanctioned Oklahoma's actions as long as equal facilities were offered. This was a setback for equality.[20] But in challenging the University of Oklahoma, Marshall not only questioned the efficacy of separate but equal facilities, he also hinted at the value of intellectual exchange across racial lines. A generation and a half later this would become the cornerstone of the diversity argument, calling for the limited use of race in admissions decisions.

During the 1940s, however, the challenge remained: breaking through the walls of segregation that fortified Jim Crow's fortress. No southern state allowed blacks to attend schools with whites, even after black and white soldiers returned home in triumph, having vanquished Nazi and Fascist armies in Europe and Asia. Most African Americans hoped for a double victory, one abroad and one at home. They found instead that change came only after a demand.[21]

Heman Sweatt, a postal worker in Texas, aspired to attend law school. Only twenty-three blacks had licenses to practice law in the state, as compared to 7,701 whites. He wouldn't settle for just any law school; he wanted to attend the state's most prestigious school, the University of Texas at Austin. It, however, barred blacks. Like other southern states, it offered to establish a black school at one of the existing colleges for Negroes. In fact, the state legislature pledged $3 million for a brand-new university for blacks, beginning with funds for a law school.

From the moment he applied for admission in 1946 until the Supreme Court heard his case on appeal in 1950, Sweatt insisted that he wanted to attend the University of Texas and no other school. The state mounted a vigorous defense of separate-but-equal policies. Marshall and his associates charted a legal defense that put the value of segregated education on trial. Drawing on legal and social science scholars, the NAACP asked what constituted a vital learning environment. NAACP experts openly rejected the social myth of blacks' inherent intellectual inferiority and the societal benefits of segregation. Anticipating questions that would become of supreme importance two generations later, University of Pennsylvania Law School dean Earl Harrison, in response to cross-examination by state attorneys, remarked that "a very important facility of a modern law school consists of one's classmates. In other words, it isn't enough to have a good professor. It is equally essential that there be a well-rounded, representative group of students in the classroom." A classroom of the making proposed by the state lacked this critical diversity, Harrison asserted. Nonetheless, the state court upheld the separate-but-equal approach. The postal worker continued his duties while his case snaked through the court system.

In nearby Oklahoma, meanwhile, the scene switched from the professional school to graduate school. Looking for an unassailable target, the NAACP agreed to represent sixty-eight-year-old George McLaurin. McLaurin, who held a master's degree, wanted a doctorate in education and applied to the University of Oklahoma, which rejected his application. McLaurin was an ideal candidate for Marshall and the NAACP because his age deflected the bugaboo of interracial marriage and dating. And given his seniority, delay, such as would be required to construct a separate facility for him, could forever cancel McLaurin's dream of a doctorate.

The NAACP skipped the state court system and appealed directly to a three-judge tribunal of the district court. In August 1948 the district court ordered the university and the state of Oklahoma to admit McLaurin, which it did. He received, thereafter, the worst kind of special treatment. Under the revised state law McLaurin could attend graduate school at the university but on a segregated basis. He would sit in a specially roped off section of class, the library, and the dining hall. If McLaurin was to learn, he would do so without benefit of free and full access to all of the university's resources, especially other students. He alone had the additional task of bearing the heavy cross of race.

The Supreme Court announced its position in both the *Sweatt* and *McLaurin* cases in the summer of 1950. Carefully dodging the matter of *Plessy,* the Vinson Court decided in favor of both men, while upholding segregation. In *Sweatt* the Court ruled that only by attending the University of Texas could he achieve the benefit of an equal education. And, contrary to the outcome in *Sipuel,* it ruled a state could not fulfill its constitutional responsibility through the maintenance of segregated law schools. *McLaurin,* the Court said, raised another constitutional matter. Individuals retained the right to associate with whomever they chose, but the state could not introduce measures that barred such interaction.[22] Thus, it outlawed roped classrooms, separate tables, and other state-mandated acts of segregation in university settings. For those hoping for a sweeping reversal of *Plessy* this was not the day. It would come four years later in the *Brown* decision. On this day the Court tracked closely to precedent, extending additional rights to blacks as citizens without overturning half a century of practice.

The *Brown v. Board of Education of Topeka* decision in 1954 did mark a fundamental break. What the Vinson Court found difficult to say, the Warren Court unanimously said: separate but equal was unconstitutional. While *Brown* addressed elementary and secondary schools most explicitly, its implications reached beyond to the collegiate and postbaccalaureate years. More than twenty years of higher education litigation played a pivotal role in shaping the *Brown* opinion. Those earlier cases established the idiocy of segregation, the role of social science in the battle to understand the consequences of racism, and the unflinching truth that all students benefited from a truly integrated learning environment.

On the Road to Bakke

Opposition to *Brown* was swift and venomous. Southern newspapers predicted the fall of the Union, an upsurge in interracial marriage, and a pronounced fraying of the social fabric. Schools across Virginia closed for a year or two in most vicinities and as long as seven years in Prince Edwards County. Arkansas Governor Orval Faubus's decision to oppose desegregation in Little Rock led to a classic confrontation between the governor and President Dwight Eisenhower. In the end the president was forced to send troops under federal command to protect nine young African Americans whose commitment to change brought them into ugly confrontation with hate-spewing mobs of white parents who violently rejected the idea of desegregated schools.

The story of the 1950s and 1960s civil rights movement is all too often remembered as the story of the heroic actions of men and women such as Rosa Parks, Martin Luther King, JoAnn Robinson, and John Lewis. Less attention focuses on the schoolchildren across the nation who found themselves on the battle lines. From 1954, when the Supreme Court declared *Plessy* null and void, through 1955, when the courts directed the South to desegregate with all deliberate speed, until 1969–71, when most southern states finally desegregated, massive resistance, interposition, and other measures of evasion dominated. Across the South lawyers visited federal courthouses to complain that "all deliberate speed" seemed on a slow train to nowhere. From Virginia to Mississippi many schools were not effectively desegregated until 1970. Moreover, that first generation, those born just as the Court rendered its *Brown* decision, had the unique experience of being the first and in some places the only to experience truly desegregated, if not integrated, classrooms. By the 1980s white flight coupled with the rise of Christian academies to resegregate classrooms north and south.[23]

Some will argue somewhat extravagantly that the nation has spent too many resources for too long a time on desegregation. A few openly daydream about the good old days when all was simple and everyone knew his or her place. Yet few readily acknowledge how recently change in American educational opportunities has come. As late as the early 1960s the University of Michigan used photos to pair freshmen roommates by race and gender. Only six or seven years before the *Bakke* decision did elementary and secondary schools across the South desegregate. Black students at historically white colleges, especially in the South, could be counted on two hands rather than by the hundreds. The average black and white American born in 1955 who lived in the South would have spent the majority of their schooling in segregated schools (typically nine years in segregated schools and at most three in desegregated environments).

A literate group of conservatives, backed by a sizable hidden army, opposed the change in their midst. Editorials decried the federal government's attack on a way of life, exposing once again the rift between those who favored states' rights and local sovereignty over national protections backed by the U.S. Constitution. Entire school systems, in fact, shut down to forestall the order to desegregate classrooms. Most important, a number of conservative activists channeled their efforts, aided by a few foundations, in the creation of a select number of focused think tanks and academy-liberated public intellectuals. The American Enterprise Institute, for example, was founded in 1943, "dedicated to preserving and strengthening the foundations of freedom—limited government, private enterprise, vital cultural and political institutions, and a strong foreign policy and national defense—through scholarly research, open debate, and publications." Three decades later financial support from beer magnate Joseph Coors gave rise to the Heritage Foundation, which says its mission is "to formulate and promote conservative public policies based on the principles of free enterprise, limited government, individual freedom, traditional American values, a strong defense." Over the course of the next half century this emerging group became known as the New Right. They would become formidable foes of those who had pushed for equality and civil rights in the period after World War II. More than anything, they came to oppose the creation, implementation, and extension of a public policy called affirmative action.[24]

During and after World War II the federal government, often pressured by blacks, introduced federal regulations or policies to police job discrimination. The pattern began with Roosevelt's creation of the Committee on Fair Employment Practices in 1941. Known as the FEPC, this body investigated charges of racial, gender, and religious discrimination in employment during the war. Many states followed with their own committees on fair employment, which in turn benefited many of the migrants who flocked into the nation's cities after 1945.

Governmental monitoring of hiring discrimination did not end with the conclusion of the war. As table 1 outlines, Democratic and Republican presidents alike issued executive orders from 1941 to 1961 to demonstrate their concerns for racial discrimination, especially by members of federal agencies. Few of these agencies had enforcement units, but their existence did allow for governmental monitoring of federal agencies and contractors.

The very first mention of affirmative action as a possible public policy program came in 1961 (although the phrase originated in 1935). On March 6 of that year President John F. Kennedy signed Executive Order 10925, which created the Committee on Equal Employment Opportunity. In that executive order he mandated that projects with federal funds "take affirmative action" to ensure hiring and promotion practices free of discrimination. Three years later the U.S. Congress signed into law the Civil Rights Act of 1964. This legislation prohibited all forms of discrimination based on race, color, religion, and national origins. The order and the act were in direct response to the objective finding that race did matter in American life and opportunity, and that some were indeed victimized by racism.[25]

This understanding gained more traction the next year, when President Lyndon Johnson, in the graduation speech at Howard University, made clear that passage of the Civil Rights Act alone would not ameliorate the lingering effects of discrimination and prejudice. Johnson told those gathered on that June day,

TABLE 1. Executive Orders on Affirmative Action, 1941–61

Executive Order	Effect	President (Party)	Year
8802	Established Fair Employment Practices Commission	Roosevelt (Democrat)	1941
9346	Recreated Fair Employment Practices Commission	Roosevelt (Democrat)	1943
9980	Created Fair Employment Board within Civil Service Commission	Truman (Democrat)	1948
10308	Created 11-person Committee on Government Compliance	Truman (Democrat)	1951
10479	Created 15-person President's Committee on Government Contracts	Eisenhower (Republican)	1953
10925	Created President's Committee on Equal Employment Opportunity	Kennedy (Democrat)	1961

Source: Adapted from John David Skrentny, *The Ironies of Affirmative Action* (Chicago: University of Chicago Press, 1996), 113–14.

You do not wipe away the scars of centuries by saying: "now, you are free to go where you want. Do as you desire, and choose the leaders you please." You do not take a man who for years has been hobbled by chains, liberate him, bring him to the starting line of a race, saying, "you are free to compete with all the others," and still justly believe you have been completely fair. . . . This is the next and more profound stage of the battle for civil rights. We seek not just freedom but opportunity—not just legal equity but human ability—not just equality as a right and a theory, but equality as a fact and a result.

Three months later Johnson put his pen behind his words and on September 24, 1965, signed Executive Order 11246. That order went further than any effort to date in establishing the federal government commitment to the general notion of "affirmative action." Johnson, without absolute clarification, instructed contractors to take affirmative action in the employment and hiring of minorities. Although he did not spell out in precise terms what affirmative action meant, he did send a clear signal that traditional avenues of hiring and employment were to come under greater scrutiny, with different results expected. This pen stroke catalyzed the debate that continues to this day about how to insure opportunity for all in such a way that race is not an invidious distinction.[26]

It was Executive Order 11246, issued by President Lyndon Johnson in 1965, which firmly established the federal government as a guiding hand in the debate about opportunity and equity. The year before Congress had passed the Civil Rights Act; that legislation forbade employment discrimination. To enforce the policy, Title VII of the Civil Rights Act created the Equal Employment Opportunity Commission (EEOC), as a five-member, bipartisan body with the power to investigate, conciliate, and resolve questions of employment discrimination. Executive Order 11246, however, established employment guidelines for federal contractors. Companies with more than fifty employees and contracts worth more than fifty thousand dollars had to develop affirmative action plans and timetables for hiring racial minorities. Some scholars attribute the growth in black economic advancement to this executive order and its multiplier effect throughout the public and private sectors.

As numerous commentators have noted over the years, ironically perhaps, it was the Republican Richard Nixon rather than the Democrat Lyndon Johnson who produced the most forceful plan for addressing workplace opportunity in American life. The American craft unions as well as the construction trades had a history of discriminatory hiring practices that was nearly one hundred years old. Brothers tended to hire brothers; fathers hired sons. Few minorities could break in, and fewer women. In Philadelphia, Pittsburgh, and other cities hostility to opening up jobs provoked explosive outbursts. Nixon, to break this juggernaut and curry political favor, instructed his labor department to seek breakthroughs in Philadelphia, with goals and timetables for improvement. President Nixon summarized the prevailing view: "We would not impose quotas, but would require federal contractors to show 'affirmative action' to meet the goals of increasing minority employment."[27]

Even before Nixon made this decision, conservatives wondered out loud if policies to improve the life chances of minorities threatened to discriminate against whites. Senator James Eastland, a very conservative Democrat from Mississippi, voiced this view during the debate over passage of the Civil Rights Act of 1964. He would say, "I know what will happen if there is a choice between hiring a White man or hiring a Negro, both having equal qualifications. I know who will get the job. It will not be the White man." Already, five years before Nixon's Philadelphia plan, whites' fear of being supplanted by blacks had entered public policy debates. Thus at the very moment federal officials strove to define affirmative action, a countereffort to temper its reach was born. The dual efforts amounted to what conservative economist Thomas Sowell labeled a conflict of visions.[28]

The public debate over education and opportunity would tra-

verse two paths. One centered on the desegregation of public schools in the North and South. A number of new measures found a public airing in the late 1960s and early 1974. Third-party candidate George Wallace, fiery governor of Alabama, commanded considerable attention as a voice for the little man. He helped the Republican Party unlock the South from the Democratic Party's grip by appealing to white voters' base concerns on matters of race, economic security, crime, and religion. Across the South in 1968 he outpolled Democratic nominee Hubert Humphrey, who came in third to Wallace and Nixon in a three-way race, and fed the belief that a new conservative core could be formed. This possibility was not lost on Republican strategist Kevin Phillips, who helped draft what became known as the Republican Party's southern strategy, an approach predicated on wresting conservative Democrats from the Democratic to the Republican Party.[29]

The red button issue of busing to achieve racial balance and diversity in public schools proved the critical wedge issue across the land. No proposal struck such a dissonant note with the white electorate as did busing. In Boston, Charlotte, Detroit, and elsewhere busing gained favor with judges seeking a solution to the lingering effects of residential segregation.[30] With few exceptions, Americans, through the 1980s—and in many areas today—lived in racially exclusive communities. The only way to correct this imbalance and eliminate school segregation was through active means such as busing. Busing, after all, had been used across the South to maintain segregation; this time it had the potential of removing it.

More than the initial debate about affirmative action, the prospects of busing white kids to previously all-black schools and blacks to previously all-white schools enraged parents, especially white parents. Yet without tackling the problem at the primary and secondary levels, advocates of equality saw little hope that postsecondary schools would ever manage to create an integrated environment.

Beyond the glare of the media's focus on busing, which was no longer just a southern issue, a new challenge to higher education emerged. By 1974, whites had begun to question any use of racial preferences in the admission process at selective universities in the United States. It did not matter that as late as the 1960s southern states such as Mississippi, Georgia, and Alabama excluded black citizens from attending public universities, or that private schools such as Rice, Duke, Vanderbilt, and Tulane had similar prohibitions. Almost forgotten, it seems, is the brutal toll efforts to desegregate southern institutions took on the minds and psyches of those pioneering few who put themselves on the line at Ole Miss, the University of Alabama, and the University of Georgia. But as journalist and desegregation pioneer Charlayne Hunter-Gault recalled, the events of the 1960s live on for those who led the fight and for the institutions they sought to change. Hunter-Gault and classmate and friend Hamilton Holmes became the first blacks to join the undergraduate class at the University of Georgia, but only after a fierce fight. A quarter of a century after her graduation, a time that allowed for some modicum of healing and distancing, she returned to campus. It was 1988, but the events of the 1960s still shaped her person, and she would tell those gathered:

> For centuries, we shared a world of courtesy and difference established on utter tragedy. As Blacks, we gave to the white world, and that world gave to us. But the gifts were ambiguous, weighted as they were with the force of unequal tradition. You were not ours, but we were yours. Then, slowly, painfully, came the furious dawn of recognition. We saw, half hidden in the blazing noonday sun, the true outline of our burden. . . . No one here today would pretend that the Old South is dead and buried, that the events of the past twenty-five years, even my presence here today, have transformed our peculiar world into one that is beyond recognition. The Confederate flag still flies in places on this campus . . . and it would still be unwise for me to spend too much time in certain municipalities a few hours' drive from here.

In confronting her own ghosts, Hunter-Gault acknowledged something else that day: everyone was history's warden; our mutual freedom and peace as a nation came only by acknowledging the connection between the past and the future.[31] After all, she had not endured taunts, threats, and recrimination to advance her life or that of friend Hamp Holmes alone. They were part of a social movement to improve the lives of many more—bright youngsters of all backgrounds who had the gifts to succeed in college.

Fifteen years after Hunter-Gault's graduation and ten years before she addressed the University of Georgia community, the question of race in college admission took another track. Minnesota native Allan Bakke, an engineer, aspired to attend medical school. He applied to a number of institutions, among them the University of California at Davis. Davis at the time had a policy of reserving sixteen slots in its entering class for racial minorities, arguing that diversifying the medical profession was essential to its mission. Bakke in turn argued that such racial preferences amounted to reverse discrimination and violated his constitutional rights.

For the first time in more than three decades the courts had to wrestle with the thorny issue of the permissible use of race in admission to graduate or professional school. Moreover, unlike plaintiffs in suits brought by the NAACP in the 1930s and 1940s, Bakke could not demonstrate a history of institutional discrimination against whites. The University of California at Davis had no history of systematically denying access to whites or of saddling whites with resource-impoverished education at segregated schools. For the first time the courts had to address the Eastland concern: could advantages for blacks and Latinos be viewed as disadvantages for some whites and thus a violation of the Constitution.

A splintered Supreme Court addressed the matter in 1978. Justice Lewis Powell wrote the prevailing opinion. Other justices concurred with or dissented from parts or all of Powell's conclusion. Powell's *Bakke* opinion guided institutions for another twenty-five years. He established that race could be a factor among others in the admission process, that each individual applicant had to be reviewed separately, that quotas were prohibited, and that diversity was a compelling state interest. The Court's majority rejected the notion that race preference could be considered to remedy past discrimination. Much had ostensibly changed in America in the years between the 1963 March on Washington and the 1978 *Bakke* decision. Thurgood Marshall, who by the latter date had joined the high court, failed in fact to convince a majority of the Court that history and race mattered and that fifteen years was too short to have corrected all the ills of centuries of slavery, racial violence, and discrimination.[32] Yet on the streets of America the debate raged as ever before as individuals assessed opportunity in their spheres of existence.

Opportunity in Postwar America

On February 25, 1967, James Farmer, former head of the Congress for Racial Equality (CORE), addressed conferees at an American Studies Conference at Lincoln University, a historically black college in Pennsylvania. Farmer came to recall his role in the civil rights struggles in the South and CORE's place in that history. He began his delivery with a brief recount of his travels and the demands of leading a major social-movement organization. He then settled into the main text of his delivery. He had just returned from Little Rock, Arkansas, the site of one of the epic showdowns in the long lists of confrontations between blacks determined to unsettle the status quo and whites who sought and fought to preserve the privileges of their whiteness. Few had forgotten the fierce determination of the young African American students who dared to integrate Central High School, or Governor Faubus's role in preserving segregation, or President Eisenhower's resort to federal intervention. This time, however, Farmer set out on a mission more humble than toasting the young. He simply wanted to know how things had changed in Little Rock, ten years later. He happened upon an old acquaintance, the kind of everyday person whose life amounts to little more than a footnote in history, if that. Farmer's informant looked at him with real sincerity and said, "Brother Farmer, everything has changed, but everything remains the same. Yes, I can now buy a hot dog at that lunch counter. Big deal." Farmer's friend didn't end his critique there, however. He added, "Yes, I can go downtown and check into a hotel, if I had the money, which I don't. I have been out of work for six months. And furthermore, if I go three miles outside the city, I won't know that there ever was a Civil Rights Act of 1964. And yes, we can sit on the front seat of the bus. We can go to the theater and sit in the audience; we can buy a hot dog and a hamburger. Everything has changed but everything remains the same."[33]

James Farmer's friend captured the pessimism and optimism in a long moment in American history. Affirmative action policies grew out of that moment. They sought to extend a helping hand to some and an avenue to mobility to many. Even by 1967, notwithstanding the personal distress of the Little Rock resident, progress had been made. In 1939, 42.5 percent of all employed black males worked in agriculture, overwhelmingly in the South; by 1969 that percentage had shrunk to 5.3 percent. Conversely, the proportion in service, including finance, insurance, and real estate, grew from 15.8 to 21.1 percent during the same period. At the same time, the percent finding jobs in public administration jumped from 1.6 to 7.3 percent. While a full 60 percent of all employed black women labored as domestic servants in 1939, just 17.5 percent did in 1969. During the same period black women saw sizable increases in clerical and sales positions, as operatives, and in other service (meaning nondomestic) jobs.[34]

No doubt the shift from the rural South to the urban South and North, which began in the first decades of the twentieth century and accelerated after World War II, contributed to the patterns described above. In addition, migration in the second half of the twentieth century corresponded with other important structural changes that had profound effects on the opportunity structures for many. First, significant numbers of blacks entered industrial sector jobs. Second, the mechanization of cotton production rendered the sharecropping system obsolete in many ways; fewer planters needed surplus labor to harvest crops cheaply when a one-time investment in a mechanical cotton picker could do the work of several men, women, and children. Third, movement into new employment sectors, no matter how temporary, fueled a closing of the income gap between blacks and whites. In 1939, the average black male earned 41 cents for every dollar earned by his white male counterpart. That figure inched to 48 cents in 1949 and 58 cents by 1969. For black women the climb was more dramatic. In 1939 black women earned 36 cents on the dollar, when compared to white women. By 1969 the figure was 84 cents on the dollar. While racial disparities persisted, measurable progress occurred.[35]

Nonetheless, huge pockets of racialized poverty persisted in America as of 1968–69. Too often prosperity in black households depended on one or two paychecks, with the loss of a steady job proving determinative. On the whole, black households earned considerably less than whites. More blacks lived on the fragile line between solvency and insolvency, comfort and poverty. As a result, poverty or potential poverty characterized life for many. This assessment validated the claims of the Little Rock resident who bleakly noted he could now buy food at any lunch counter in the city, only he lacked the financial means—not the spirit or desire. Armed with nothing more than personal experience, his assessment explained a great deal by the end of the 1960s.

Of course neither social critique nor social policy ended in 1969. Progress continued to be made. According to a recent assessment, 93 percent of blacks and 65 percent of whites lived in poverty in 1939—that is, during the final years of the depression. Wages increased, benefits (health insurance, etc.) expanded, and poverty rates dipped significantly over the next three and a half decades.

Figures for 1974 show that 30 percent of blacks and just 9 percent of whites lived below the poverty line. As the nation struggled through a recession in the 1980s, the poverty rate increased, but the differential remained pretty much at 1974 levels. Thus while opportunities for blacks grew between the depression and the Great Society, race continued to make a difference. And a narrowing of the income gap did little to diminish the gap in wealth.[36]

Racial differences had a disproportionate effect on children. As late as 1985 nearly half (44 percent) of black children lived in poverty, compared to 16 percent of whites. If one removes governmental assistance and other transfer payments from the calculations, nearly two-thirds of all black children spent some portion of the first ten years of their lives in poor households. Of course there is a direct correlation between the increase in female-headed households and poverty. While we can debate whether a female-headed household is a priori dysfunctional, there is little doubt that such households are the sites of large pockets of poverty in the United States (by 1985, 75 percent of black children and 42 percent of white children lived in female-headed households). Some economists have warned, however, that the real increase in poverty for all racial groups stemmed from a real decline in earnings between the 1970s and 1980s, with low-wage workers hurt the most. Nor was poverty evenly distributed. Among whites the poor were spread from non-metropolitan areas to suburbs to the inner city. With the mass movement of blacks to cities and the corresponding demographic shift, the bulk of black poverty was housed in the central city.[37]

Access to the full benefits of American life seemed tantalizingly closer for the post-1960s generation than any cohort since Emancipation. But what much of the scholarship and commentary on the struggle for civil rights often ignores is the most essential: blacks sought more than just equality, they sought equity. The pursuit of equity, many understood, meant state action to level the playing field, when and where needed. The appearance of inequality could lead to the achievement of equality. Equity meant becoming equal.

In everyday language, NAACP President Ben Hooks often referenced the staggering of the starting blocks in a 400-meter race. Each racer had an assigned starting place. Although from the casual glance, it appeared that the outside runner had an advantage over the runner in lane one, such was not the case. That is certainly the subtext of James Farmer's friend's comment. He understood that the removal of segregation signs was an important but incomplete achievement. He wasn't alone. Martin Luther King reached a similar conclusion in his last years, as he doggedly pushed for a poor people's campaign. This sentiment crisscrossed the words and deeds of those who crafted the Black Manifesto and a number of other utterances from the 1960s and 1970s. If one looks closely, the cry for equity even existed in the songs of the civil rights struggle. Freedom to live where they chose, eat where they liked, earn what their education and skills would produce, and to do so unshackled by the heavy cross of racism animated the songs. Oftentimes meaning was shrouded in the language of misdirection, but when reanalyzed the songs revealed a collection of individuals for whom democracy hinged on equitable and not just equal access to the nation's bounty. Was this true for all that participated? Undoubtedly not. Was this a part of the lexicon of social relations that shaped public policy then and now? The answer is unquestionably, yes.[38]

Debate over Affirmative Action

The debate about affirmative action in the United States is fundamentally about how to reconcile the tension between the need to include and the desire to limit that inclusion. In fact, it can be argued that affirmative action represented a fairly conservative state innovation. Critics, of course, emphasized the excesses: poorly qualified job seekers securing hiring preferences because of their race or gender; selective colleges and universities admitting woefully underprepared students because they were racial minorities;

objectively weaker firms winning bids to fulfill a tacit quota. While some advocated the abolition of standards and hired folks of questionable qualifications, by all accounts the exaggerated anecdotes captured the broadest headlines. In the 1960s Republicans and Democrats alike feared the America they saw on the television screens each night—riots, racial confrontations, an open questioning of authority, and bleak, unvarnished portraits of despair and hopelessness in large pockets of urban and rural America. Thus it was not a calculated overthrow of the established order that led President Lyndon Johnson to call for federally supported state access to opportunity. Johnson understood that individuals with a stake in society made better—and perhaps quieter—citizens. Nor was this perspective lost on the Republican president Richard Nixon, who embraced and expanded affirmative action policies, especially in the employment sectors. For a moment, in fact, it appeared that an agreement had emerged to ameliorate past injustices by consciously considering race, among other attributes, as a positive for blacks as it had served for whites.

During the period between 1968 and 1978 affirmative action policy began to take shape in several specific areas—in education, employment, and promotions. Although some objected to what unfolded, the United States had previously preserved certain benefits for discrete groups. The most heralded example came after World War II. This time members of Congress preserved special status for the millions of returning soldiers. They received extra points on civil service exams, attractive grants for attending colleges, assistance in purchasing homes, and other advantages denied to civilians, and even previous veterans. This G.I. Bill of Rights became known as "veterans' preferences," writes John David Skrentny, "rather than hidden with an ambiguous term like *affirmative action.*"[39]

While it may be argued that the phrase itself was ambiguous, the intent was crystal clear to most Americans. Certainly by the mid-1970s most knew that affirmative action policies were adopted to address past and current inequities in education, employment, and promotions. Had a consensus emerged about the efficacy of this policy? Certainly not. As a bevy of social scientists noted by the mid-1980s, many whites harbored great ambivalence, if not outrage, at the idea of blacks getting more than they supposedly deserved. Scholars complained of reverse discrimination, blacks of tokenism, and conservatives of all races of the bastardization of standards. The journalist Nicholas Lemann recently suggested that the outcry over the last fifteen years is not surprising given the quick endorsement of affirmative action by policymakers and politicians of both parties by the mid-1970s. He contends that it was the *Bakke* case, which centered on Allan Bakke's claim that the University of California at Davis Medical School had set aside sixteen slots for racial minorities with lower test scores and grade point averages, that initiated the current period of public debate.[40]

Lemann may be only partially correct. For more than two decades Americans have discussed the value of set-aside programs, preferences in hiring, promotions, and the awarding of contracts. Case law in the United States is replete with examples of jurists, opposing lawyers, and clients debating the importance of continuing or eliminating programs that came under the umbrella of affirmative action. Since the 1970s a few social scientists have gained prominence by asserting with renewed vigor that no matter what social policies are adopted black Americans lack the intellectual acumen to compete successfully with whites and Asians. From William Shockley and Richard Jensen to Richard Herrnstein and Charles Murray, a kind of biological determinism was mobilized to undermine a range of social policies, including affirmative action.[41]

In the second half of the 1990s poll data reflect a great degree of public ambivalence about the efficacy of race-based preferences, with responses turning as much on phrasing and word choice as in a full rejection of policies and practices that allow race or gender to be among a number of factors taken into consideration for admission to colleges or in job selection. However, Myrdal's earlier conclusion that race and place in a democratic society amounted to a national dilemma pulses with as much currency as it did five decades ago. An implicit assumption in the earlier study warrants closer analysis. The difficulty with affirmative action is not that critics and proponents cannot cite examples of successes and excesses. With such policies, with as many variations as have occurred over the last three decades, there are bound to be examples of both. Nor should policymakers lose sight of questions of morality, fairness, and justice. A profound commitment to fairness has been a stated objective of liberal democracies for some time. Still, those same policymakers should seek to balance overall social benefit against individual complaints of injury. In the United States this balancing act is further complicated by the nation's very diversity. For example, there has always been one black America and many African American communities. Similarly, all white Americans do not possess the same social, political, or economic privileges. If anything a fuller consideration of diversity may aid the debate that Lemann thinks Americans must have; it will certainly show that no society can escape its history, although its members can design their future.

Implications from the Michigan Example

In 1997 the conservative legal advocacy group Center for Individual Rights (CIR), backed by a few Michigan state legislators, and financed by what appears to be an interlocking group of foundations opposed to affirmative action, launched a campaign directed at the University of Michigan. A handful of Republicans in the state had attempted to get the legislature to pass provisions abolishing affirmative action in admission to the state's leading institutions, most notably the University of Michigan, Ann Arbor. Seizing the language of individual rights, the attack on the university came from some at least who believed that race should be an inconsequential factor.

Following a spate of racist and racially insensitive incidents in the late 1980s, university officials, especially newly named president James Duderstadt, championed a greater effort to increase the numbers of racial minorities and women in faculty and staff positions and students enrolled in the institution's undergraduate programs. Duderstadt labeled his effort the Michigan Mandate, and from 1988 through his resignation as president in 1995 he insisted that all units report their successes and failures in diversifying the campus. This approach became a lightning rod for those opposed to and supportive of the university's objective.

Soon after Lee Bollinger was named president of Michigan in 1997 three Republican legislators placed ads in newspapers statewide inviting white students who believed that race played a factor in their failure to gain admission to the university to contact them. According to published reports more than five hundred replied. The three legislators took this route after failing to garner support for legislative injunctions on either side of the political aisle. Neither Republicans nor Democrats had an interest in attacking this socially explosive issue.[42]

To a certain degree conservative activists had claimed the language and style of the old civil rights activists as their own. They were now out to eliminate the use of race in critical areas of American life. They were out to protect individual rights over group preferences. They were willing to mobilize a population through direct appeals to potential plaintiffs. When the NAACP used such tactics in the 1930s, 1940s, and 1950s, whites, especially in the South, branded them outside agitators. Such charges failed to materialize this time around. Echoes of Senator Eastland still reverberated across the social landscape of America more than three decades later: black gain would amount to white loss. Scores of whites earnestly believed that racial preferences must have accounted for the rejection or deferral letters they received; otherwise, how do you explain that a black or Latino had gotten into Michigan and they had not. Nor would sophisticated statistical explanations mollify them. It didn't matter that the elimination of all underrepresented minorities from the pool of applicants would have only marginally increased their likelihood of admission. The reaction was visceral and individual. They were out and someone else was in. They had come to believe that color-blind and race-neutral meant the same thing.

CIR settled on three individuals in two separate cases. Jennifer Gratz and Patrick Hamacher complained that the undergraduate admission process at the university unfairly discriminated against them. Meanwhile, Barbara Grutter brought suit against the university's law school, which had an entirely different admission process, requirements, and pool of applicants. She too alleged that the use of race in the admission process discriminated against her and favored blacks, American Indians, and Latinos.

My colleagues Patricia Gurin and Jeffrey Lehman will detail the educational benefits of diversity and the legal rationale adopted by the University of Michigan in the challenge brought forth by Grutter, Gratz, and Hamacher. It is important to remember, however, a commitment to diversity originated with the institution's founding and changed in scope and breadth as the society grew and developed. As early as 1887 a *Harper's Weekly* article observed,

> The most striking feature of the University [of Michigan] is the broad and liberal spirit in which it does its work. Women are admitted to all departments on equal terms with men; the doors of the University are open to all applicants who are properly qualified, from whatever part of the world they may come.[43]

"Inclusiveness" has been part of the university's modus operandi, at least tacitly, almost from the beginning.

The university's first international student (a Canadian) was admitted in 1843; the first black males (both from Detroit), in 1868, with absolutely no fuss or fanfare. On the other hand, there was considerable controversy over the admission of the first women in 1870, but, under interim president Henry Simmons Frieze, a resolution by the board of regents that the university was open to any person who "possesses the requisite literary and moral qualifications" settled the matter. Michigan, however, was by no means the first institution of higher learning in the Midwest to admit women: as early as 1834, Oberlin College was enrolling both women and black students. The first black woman enrolled in 1878, and by the late 1800s, Michigan was a place where at least some qualified black students could earn an education.[44]

The University of Michigan was never a utopia, however. For most years the numbers of students of color could be counted on both hands. So despite a long tradition of accepting students of color, that tradition reflected a passive approach rather than an active effort to attract women and students of color; hence, the numbers of those students remained relatively small in comparison to total enrollment. Predictably, such small representation brought concomitant difficulties. In 1940, for example, when black students represented only 1 percent of the total student enrollment, they reported financial problems because of a lack of financial resources and because most available jobs went to white students. Perceptions accounted for much. Black students in particular complained of being treated differently and of an inadequate social life.

During much of the twentieth century, women and members of racial and ethnic groups were faced with various kinds of legal and social exclusion, not least of all in the realm of education. Because education, in a very real sense, is what opens the door to opportunity, it was not really surprising that education should be at the forefront of the most important civil rights decision of the twentieth century, *Brown v. Board of Education.* Nevertheless, for nearly two decades following the *Brown* decision, educational institutions—especially colleges and graduate schools—remained predominantly white and male. Only after enactment of affirmative action measures in the late 1960s and early 1970s did the enrollment percentages for students of color, especially black students, begin to show significant improvement.[45]

I have already mentioned Johnson's Executive Order 11246, which is generally credited with launching what we have come to call the affirmative action movement. The order required federal contractors to take "affirmative action" to ensure equality of employment opportunity without regard to race, religion and national origin, and was expanded in 1968 to include gender. What made the order different from its predecessors, however, was that it was turned over to the Labor Department for administration. This meant, in turn, that the provisions of the order could now be enforced. It also meant that colleges and universities receiving funding from the federal government were subject to the affirmative action provisions.

With the implementation of President Johnson's executive order came the first real pressure for colleges and universities throughout the country to increase not only their enrollment of underrepresented students, but also their hiring of faculty and staff. The effect was certainly felt at the University of Michigan, which began to take an increasingly proactive stance in making the university more inclusive.

The 1960s and 1970s were eras of increasing student activism and unrest, fueled not only by major civil rights actions (the march on Selma, for example), but by increasing U.S. military involvement in Vietnam. Between February and April 1970 the University of Michigan campus was torn by a series of university-wide confrontations. The list included a strike against classes, with considerable pressure put on faculty and students to participate, and by the Black Action Movement (BAM), which had a stated goal of increasing black enrollment to 10 percent of total enrollment by 1973.

By 1975, the goal of 10 percent black enrollment still had not been reached, and students protested once again (BAM II). The goal of 10 percent was not actually reached until 1976, and even then continued to grow slowly (by 1984, minority students represented only 11 percent of total enrollment). In 1987, at a time when campus feelings against apartheid in South Africa animated significant numbers of students, the issue of minority enrollment resurfaced, sparking what some called the BAM III movement. Most notably, continued failure by the university to fulfill its commitment to increase black enrollment led to a blockade of the Michigan Student Union and to sit-ins in the Fleming Administration Building.

Since the last BAM strike in 1987, the University of Michigan has vigorously pursued a policy of ensuring that more members of underrepresented groups are admitted to the university and that they have the opportunity to participate fully in the life of the institution. Steps taken include providing substantial financial support to these students at all degree levels, developing the necessary administrative infrastructures to support affirmative action and equal opportunity, and designing an extensive array of recruiting and retention programs.[46]

In 1988, the university announced its strategic plan, President Duderstadt's Michigan Mandate, which was designed to ensure that all racial and ethnic groups would be full participants in the life of the university. The fundamental principle of the mandate was that the university should become a leader in creating a multicultural community that could serve as a model for society as well as for higher education. An integral part of the mandate was the Michigan Agenda, which outlined a similar series of strategic actions designed to produce gender equity and a university environment that would foster the success of women, be they students, faculty, or staff.

By the time Grutter, Gratz, and Hamacher brought suit in 1997, "minority" enrollment was 25 percent, including Asian Americans, and females totaled 47 percent of all students. The numbers fail to address the true benefits of diversity for majority and minority student alike. The lawsuits, ironically, did force the university to clarify what it had been doing and why, and to articulate a rationale for the educational benefits of diversity. This close examination is good for all sectors of society and may prove the most enduring legacy of CIR's challenges. Fundamentally, improving access is a part of the process of enabling interaction. After all how do you achieve sufficient numbers of students from various backgrounds if you are asked to ignore the entire person? The courts answered that you could do so as long as a mechanistic approach is not taken. That the undergraduate admissions staff had looked and reviewed each of the more than fourteen thousand applications each year was lost on all but two members of the Supreme Court. The majority interpreted evidence in a manner that suggested the university's practices at the undergraduate level were too formulaic. The Court upheld that while affirmative action is the policy, diversity is the goal. And building an inclusive diverse society is as paramount today as it was a generation ago. As one national commission noted, "The current scope of affirmative action programs is best understood as an outgrowth and continuation of our national effort to remedy subjugation of racial and ethnic minorities and of women—subjugation in place at our nation's founding and still the law of the land within the lifetime of 'baby-boomers.'"[47]

Conclusion

More than a decade since she defined herself as black, my daughter's thoughts on race in America have evolved. She is now poised to compete for a seat in the 2004 freshman class at some of the nation's most selective institutions. She has amassed a cumulative GPA of about 3.8 at a leading area prep school, competitive test scores, significant work experience, and a varsity letter. She has also experienced the divorce of parents, bouts of depression, and general adolescent angst.

Nonetheless, she frequently complains that we spend too much time talking about race. She chafes when her younger brother reads a social situation through the color-tinted lenses of race and history. She begs him to stop. She's equally critical of white friends, especially males, who believe race is an artifice that could never have had a bearing on her life and her experiences. Their inability to see race is as palpable for her as her brother's quick resort to racial explanation.

For my daughter, race matters more than she would like at times, and that's the conundrum she and we face. Some could rightly ask why an admissions counselor would pay any attention to my daughter's racial and ethnic background. She grew up in upper-middle-class circumstances with a father who is a faculty member and administrator. She has certainly had advantages; some would even cry privileges. Why should she get any boosts?

Yet she has never had the privilege of living in a race-neutral or color-blind world. Dates, friendships, expectations, and obligations have been shaped by her place on America's racial pentagram. Some of these encounters have been painfully hurtful; others enriching and they have afforded an opportunity to grow. Still Ann Arbor is by no means the rest of the country. The cocoon-like environment of a college town can afford an unrealistic portrait of what's ahead and how race may or may not figure in the equation.

If diversity is the key, ignoring race would amount to the greatest contrivance, even for my somewhat privileged daughter. Universities and colleges have asked, and received, the right to review the entire applicant. In that way we operate like other sectors of society. At the scene of a crime the officer asks the witness for all bits of information, no matter how trivial. One cannot imagine a witness failing to note the race, gender, height, age, or weight of a would-be suspect if they had that information and were free to give it. It is the officer's job to sort between the important and the insignificant. For decades now universities have so functioned. They receive mounds of information on each applicant, and from there they go through an exhaustive review of the characteristics that make one individual more compelling for inclusion in the freshman class over another. It has never been just about grade point averages or test scores, nor should it ever. What a young person scores on one day's test or how much they achieved in high school is at best a loose proxy for future achievement. Noncognitive factors such as creativity, perseverance, resilience, cooperation, and curiosity are equally important; as too are family background, resourcefulness, drive, and dedication.

Truth be told, selective universities and colleges take few risks on truly marginal students. If they do, typically they are star athletes or musicians or politically connected. Moreover, the University of Michigan and others like it have long tried to have race count as but one of many factors in the admission process. The university knows the folly of admitting a kid just because he or she is black, brown, or red. And even attorneys for the Center for Individual Rights admitted that *all* students admitted to the university are qualified. So the red herring of admitting an unqualified black or Latino student over a qualified white applicant is a shibboleth designed to inflame more than inform.

It would be foolish to believe legal challenge or threat will not produce a change in behavior. Without stretching credulity, one can imagine this as a desired outcome. Threatening letters from the Center for Equal Opportunity, for example, led Princeton and MIT to open summer research opportunity programs to all students, irrespective of race, and produced consternation across other campuses. Perhaps we have reached a stage when such programs should have a broader constituency. Still the imperative that gave rise to them has not disappeared. The country desperately needs the intellectual capital found within all segments of the population. Demographic shifts in the composition of America's school-age population increase the power of the realization. Failure to identify and nurture such talent has profound implications. Sweeping change or incremental recision seems the strategy of affirmative action opponents. And conceivably race and class will be indexed on a kind of sliding scale, with race functioning as a plus factor for first-generation college students more than others.[48]

Whether that takes twenty-five years, as Justice Sandra Day O'Connor hopes, or much longer, as Justices Ruth Bader Ginsburg and Stephen Breyer fear, there is no way of eluding the conclusion that history matters in the contemporary debate about race, social policy, and higher education. When the NAACP began its assault on segregation in the 1930s, it fought for all black Americans deprived access to various social institutions. NAACP lawyers leaned on the Fourteenth Amendment's guarantee of equal protection under the law, which had been crafted to check the excesses of the majority. The cases in the law books bear the names of Sweatt, McLaurin, Sipuel, Gaines, and Murray, but behind them stood others systematically denied pathways to opportunity because of their race. In telling contrast neither Grutter, Gratz, nor Hamacher represented such a class. The majority of admittees, students, and alumni of the University of Michigan remain, as they have been for decades, overwhelmingly white. Thus the Court, the university, and society have to balance race as a positive and a negative force in everyday life.

The University of Michigan in these legal cases understood and appreciated its place in the nation's history. It mounted a successful defense of affirmative action before the Supreme Court because colleges and universities have a vaunted role in building a diverse democracy. For a few choice years they welcome the world's brightest and invite them to learn in close proximity. Many have assumptions questioned, viewpoints challenged, and long-held beliefs tested. They learn and make the most of the environment. Others hunker down and find that school narrows rather than expands their outlook on the world. Whatever the outcome, nothing can substitute for the grand experiment that is college education. The production of a talented and informed citizenry is as critical to the nation's future as ever before, and including a broad cross-section of Americans in those conversations is critical. That is why affirmative action, as one public policy option, commands a longer life than opponents dare claim. Its maintenance is not about the weakening of standards or the fraying of interracial relations. No matter how many times we click our heels and wish it were not so, race and history matter in the lives of all Americans. Maybe one day that will be less so. But at no time should we trade an honest exploration of our past for a Disney-like substitute. Tackling the history of race is the only way to build a diverse, plural democracy. And collectively that remains our shared responsibility.

The Evolving Language of Diversity and Integration in Discussions of Affirmative Action from *Bakke* to *Grutter*

Jeffrey S. Lehman

In December 1997, Barbara Grutter brought a lawsuit challenging the constitutionality of the University of Michigan Law School's admissions policy. In June 2003 the United States Supreme Court issued its opinion in *Grutter v. Bollinger,* definitively rejecting that challenge. I served as dean of the Law School throughout the five-and-one-half-year litigation, and my role gave me many opportunities to reflect on the different factors that have made affirmative action such a difficult issue.

As one of the university's public representatives throughout the litigation, I was often called upon to speak and write about the case. It was important to me that I be able to speak consistently— describing the issues in the same terms, regardless of whether my immediate audience was supportive or critical of our admissions policy. It was important that I be able to speak consistently with our published admissions policy. It was important that I be able to speak consistently with our court submissions. And it was important that I be able to speak in a way that I felt authentically captured the complexities of the issues.

As I returned to the topic again and again, I found this to be an exceptionally challenging exercise. What made the topic so difficult was the way in which Justice Powell's opinion in *Bakke* had restricted the terrain on which university officials could address affirmative action. A language that speaks only about the "educational benefits of diversity" offers an incomplete vocabulary for talking and thinking about race and higher education. Over the duration of the lawsuit, therefore, I heard my own voice evolve.

Most Americans resonate with the ideal of color blindness—that public and private institutions, and even individuals, should not allow their conduct toward a person to be influenced by that person's race or ethnicity. That ideal has found expression in many corners of our society, most notably in the legal doctrine that has interpreted the Equal Protection Clause of the Fourteenth Amendment to the United States Constitution. Under that doctrine, departures from color blindness are not necessarily unlawful, but (to use the legal terms of art) they are always "suspect"; they demand justification in the form of a "compelling interest."

As I worked alongside many others to explain why, in the context of university admissions, carefully crafted departures from the ideal of color blindness can be both lawful and appropriate, I found myself referring more and more to an ideal that seems today to carry more resonance with most Americans than the pedagogic notion of diversity. More and more, I invoked the vocabulary of integration. The word *diversity* can feel somewhat one-dimensional, connoting only a property of racial heterogeneity that may or may not exist in a particular place at a particular moment in time. At least today, the word *integration* does a better job of capturing the special importance to our country of undoing the damaging legacy of laws and norms that artificially separated citizens from one another on the basis of race. The enduring scars left by that history pose the greatest practical challenge to our nation's prosperity and, for many, to its democratic legitimacy.[1]

A close reading of the Supreme Court's opinion upholding our admissions policy reveals that, over the span of twenty-five years from *Bakke* to *Grutter,* the Court underwent a similar evolution. Justice Powell's opinion in *Bakke* was succeeded by an opinion for the Court that drew on a more satisfying, weightier justification for universities' departure from color blindness. The "compelling interest" is about more than just pedagogy. It is about the fundamental legitimacy of America's approach to distributing educational opportunity.

In this essay, I will trace the parallel evolutions of the vocabulary of Supreme Court doctrine and my own discussions of affirmative action in my role as a law school dean. I will begin with Justice Powell's opinion in *Bakke* and end with Justice O'Connor's opinion in *Grutter.* In between, I will discuss the admissions policy adopted by the University of Michigan Law School in 1992 that became the subject of the litigation and then reflect on several of my own public statements over the course of the litigation. I will suggest that the overall movement in vocabulary over the course of the litigation—from diversity to integration, pedagogy to democratic legitimacy—is a healthy movement for constitutional doctrine, higher education, and public discussions of race and ethnicity.

Justice Powell's opinion in *Bakke* defined the legal background for university admissions policies after 1978. In his opinion, Justice Powell endorsed one particular understanding of why universities have a compelling interest in enrolling a racially diverse student body. He recognized that diversity has *pedagogic* benefits. His opinion describes an environmental condition that enhances students' opportunities to learn.

Justice Powell began with a general observation, "The atmosphere of 'speculation, experiment and creation'—so essential to the quality of higher education—is widely believed to be promoted by a diverse student body" (*Regents of the University of California v.*

Bakke, 438 U.S. 265, 312–15 (1978)). For this proposition, he relied upon the trenchant comments of the then-president of Princeton University, William Bowen:

> [A] great deal of learning occurs informally. It occurs through interactions among students of both sexes; of different races, religions, and backgrounds; who come from cities and rural areas, from various states and countries; who have a wide variety of interests, talents, and perspectives; and who are able, directly or indirectly, to learn from their differences and to stimulate one another to reexamine even their most deeply held assumptions about themselves and their world. As a wise graduate of ours observed in commenting on this aspect of the educational process, "People do not learn very much when they are surrounded only by the likes of themselves." . . .
>
> In the nature of things, it is hard to know how, and when, and even if, this informal "learning through diversity" actually occurs. It does not occur for everyone. For many, however, the unplanned, casual encounters with roommates, fellow sufferers in an organic chemistry class, student workers in the library, teammates on a basketball squad, or other participants in class affairs or student government can be subtle and yet powerful sources of improved understanding and personal growth. (*Bakke,* 312–13 n. 48, quoting Bowen, "Admissions and the Relevance of Race," *Princeton Alumni Weekly,* Sept. 26, 1977)

Justice Powell declared that a university's desire to nourish such an atmosphere of speculation implicates the values of the First Amendment, values that respect a university's interests in defining itself as an institution and in becoming the kind of school it aspires to be:

> Thus, in arguing that its universities must be accorded the right to select those students who will contribute the most to the "robust exchange of ideas," petitioner invokes a countervailing

constitutional interest, that of the First Amendment. In this light, petitioner must be viewed as seeking to achieve a goal that is of paramount importance in the fulfillment of its mission. (*Bakke*, 312–13)

He went on to endorse the idea that the existence of a diverse student body offers pedagogic benefits for professional schools as well as undergraduate colleges (*Bakke*, 313–14):

It may be argued that there is greater force to these views at the undergraduate level than in a medical school where the training is centered primarily on professional competency. But even at the graduate level, our tradition and experience lend support to the view that the contribution of diversity is substantial. In *Sweatt v. Painter*, 339 U.S., at 634, the Court made a similar point with specific reference to legal education: "The law school, the proving ground for legal learning and practice, cannot be effective in isolation from the individuals and institutions with which the law interacts. Few students and no one who has practiced law would choose to study in an academic vacuum, removed from the interplay of ideas and the exchange of views with which the law is concerned."

Physicians serve a heterogeneous population. An otherwise qualified medical student with a particular background—whether it be ethnic, geographic, culturally advantaged or disadvantaged—may bring to a professional school of medicine experiences, outlooks, and ideas that enrich the training of its student body and better equip its graduates to render with understanding their vital service to humanity.

After recognizing that this pedagogic interest in diversity can be compelling, Justice Powell went on to note that such an interest nevertheless cannot justify any and all admissions policies that promote it. A policy that categorizes students on the basis of race must do so in a manner (to use another legal term of art) that is "narrowly tailored" to the pursuit of that interest. It must honestly recognize that racial and ethnic diversity is not the only kind of diversity that has such pedagogic value. "The diversity that furthers a compelling state interest encompasses a far broader array of qualifications and characteristics of which racial or ethnic origin is but a single though important element" (*Bakke,* 315). The university must employ a capacious understanding of what constitutes "beneficial educational pluralism," consider "all pertinent elements of diversity," and "place them on the same footing for consideration, though not necessarily according them the same weight" (*Bakke,* 317). Such a policy must not insulate any applicant from comparison with all other applicants; rather, it must attempt to "treat[ ] each applicant as an individual" and evaluate that individual's "combined qualifications" for admission (*Bakke,* 318).

During the academic year 1991–92, I served as one of the junior members of a faculty committee charged with revising the Law School's admissions policy. Part of our mandate was to produce a policy that was lawful under the guidelines established by Justice Powell. We sought to develop a policy that would incorporate this pedagogic vision of diversity into a general philosophy of admissions that accurately captured our own definition of ourselves as an institution and linked our admissions process to our more general efforts to become the kind of law school we aspired to be. And we attempted to devise a system that would carry that philosophy forward into the daily work of an admissions office.

The policy begins with a paragraph that expresses complex and multiple aspirations:

> Our goal is to admit a group of students who individually and
> collectively are among the most capable students applying to

American law schools in a given year. As individuals we expect our admittees not only to have substantial promise for success in law school but also to have a strong likelihood of succeeding in the practice of law and contributing in diverse ways to the well-being of others. Michigan has many alumni who are esteemed legal practitioners, leaders of the American bar, significant contributors to legal scholarship and/or selfless contributors to the public interest. Those we admit should have the potential to follow in those traditions.

The paragraph does three important things. First, it associates Michigan with the twin ideals of "success" and "contribution." Second, it recognizes that success and contribution are to be found in widely diverse domains of endeavor. And third, it endorses the view that the admissions process entails an assessment of an individual's "promise" or "potential" to succeed and contribute.

The next paragraph of the policy relates the goals for the admissions process to the mechanisms through which law students learn—mechanisms that move far beyond the classroom and that reflect both the individual qualities of students and their dynamics as a group.

Collectively, we seek a mix of students with varying backgrounds and experiences who will respect and learn from each other. We hope our students will find in their peers both rich resources for learning and the kind of sustaining friendships that help in getting over hard times and make the good times yet more pleasant. We hope professors will see in their students one of the rewards of teaching at this school. In the classroom setting the educational experience depends in large measure upon the quality of student performance. Many law school classes depend on prepared and articulate students to advance the discussion, and in all classes perceptive, original observations can teach both faculty and students alike. We also recognize that much that is educationally valuable occurs not in the classroom but in informal conversations and in the more formal activities of numerous student organizations such as Michigan's many law journals, various ethnic-, religious-, and gender-focused groups, numerous practice-oriented and law-specialty societies and diverse political groups of the left, right and in between. As a group our students have the responsibility for maintaining and changing this vibrant extra-curricular life in ways that respond to their own needs and concerns. At the admissions stage we value people who have shown the capacity to be self-educating and to contribute to the learning of those around them.

Having framed its goals in this general manner, the admissions policy then proceeds to provide more specific guidance to the admissions office. Reflecting the individual and collective nature of the education offered by the school, it establishes two preliminary principles for admissions that consider candidates both as individuals and as members of a group. The first (individual-focused) principle is that "no applicant should be admitted unless we expect that applicant to do well enough to graduate with no serious academic problems." The second (group-focused) principle is that "a reasonable proportion of our places should go to Michigan residents, even if some have qualifications lower than those of some [rejected] applicants from outside Michigan."

The minimal principles—individual academic qualification and representation of Michigan residents—define somewhat rigid boundaries for the evaluative work of the admissions office. The remainder of the policy (which accounts for thirteen of the sixteen pages) discusses what the admissions office should do within those boundaries. That discussion unfolds in three stages, carefully tracking the vision of Justice Powell. They discuss in general terms the weight to be given the various qualities of an individual candidate. They relate those considerations to the pedagogic interest in having a class that is diverse in every sense of the word. And they situate the Law School's interest in having a racially diverse class within the frame of that broad pedagogic interest.

The first stage of the discussion of how judgment should be exercised within the boundaries of individual academic qualification and representation of Michigan residents concerns the individual student's potential to excel academically:

> We begin with the individual and the goal of maximizing competence. Our most general measure . . . of the likelihood of a distinguished legal career is success in law school as operationalized by graded law school performance. [And our] most general measure predicting graded law school performance is a composite of an applicant's LSAT score and undergraduate grade point average [known as the "index"]. . . .
>
> [T]he higher one's index score, the greater should be one's chances of being admitted. . . . Still, even the highest possible score ought not guarantee admission: imagine an applicant whose undergraduate course selection seems relentlessly dull, whose personal statements and LSAT essay are thin or incoherent, and whose letters of recommendation damn with faint praise. And even a quite low score ought not automatically deny a candidate admission: for again one can imagine dramatically offsetting considerations.
>
> When the differences in index scores are small, we believe it is important to weigh as best we can not just the index but also such file characteristics as the enthusiasm of recommenders, the quality of the undergraduate institution, the quality of the applicant's essay, and the areas and difficulty of undergraduate course selection. . . . [S]ome students will qualify for admission despite index scores that place them relatively far from the upper right corner of [a grid that plots students' undergraduate grades and test scores]. . . . [T]here are students for whom we have good reason to be skeptical of an index score based prediction.

The second stage of the discussion of how judgment should be exercised within the boundaries of individual academic qualification and representation of Michigan residents concerns the collective diversity of the class, with diversity understood in its broadest sense.

Other information in an applicant's file may add nothing about the applicant's likely LGPA beyond what may be discerned from the index, but it may suggest that that applicant has a perspective or experiences that will contribute to the diverse student body that we hope to assemble. The applicant may for example be a member of a minority group whose experiences are likely to be different from those of most students, may be likely to make a unique contribution to the bar, or may have had a successful career as a concert pianist or may speak five languages. . . .

[A]dmitting students with indices relatively far from the upper right corner . . . may help achieve that diversity which has the potential to enrich everyone's education and thus make a law school class stronger than the sum of its parts. In particular we seek to admit students with distinctive perspectives and experiences as well as students who are particularly likely to assume the kinds of leadership roles in the bar and make the kinds of contributions to society discussed in the introduction to this report. (We reiterate, however, that no student should be admitted unless his or her file as a whole leads us to expect him or her to do well enough to graduate without serious academic problems.)

There are many possible bases for diversity admissions. During the past year for example the Admissions Committee, influenced by diversity considerations, has recommended the admission of students like the following. . . .

Other bases for such admissions decisions will also come readily to mind, although different faculty members will, no doubt, think of different achievements or characteristics they would value. One might, for example, give substantial weight to an Olympic gold medal, a Ph.D. in physics, the attainment of age 50 in a class that otherwise lacked anyone over 30, or the experience of having been a Vietnamese boat person.

The third and final stage of the discussion of how judgment should be exercised within the boundaries of individual academic qualification and representation of Michigan residents concerns the importance of racial and ethnic diversity within the context of diversity understood in its broadest sense:

> There is, however, a commitment to one particular type of diversity that the school has long had and which should continue. This is a commitment to racial and ethnic diversity with special reference to the inclusion of students from groups which have been historically discriminated against, like African Americans, Hispanics and Native Americans, who without this commitment might not be represented in our student body in meaningful numbers. These students are particularly likely to have experiences and perspectives of special importance to our mission.
>
> Over the past two decades, the law school has made special efforts to increase the numbers of such students in the school. We believe that the racial and ethnic diversity that has resulted has made the University of Michigan Law School a better law school than it could possibly have been otherwise. By enrolling a "critical mass" of minority students, we have ensured their ability to make unique contributions to the character of the Law School; the policies embodied in this document should ensure that those contributions continue in the future.
>
> While one of our goals is to have substantial and meaningful racial and ethnic diversity, we do not, as we have already indicated, mean to define diversity solely in terms of racial and ethnic status. Nor are we insensitive to the competition among all students for admission to this law school.

During the litigation, much attention was paid to the term "critical mass," and whether it might somehow have been intended to smuggle a quota-based system into the policy. (It wasn't, and the Supreme Court's opinion held as much.) For purposes of this essay, however, I would like to concentrate on the first paragraph and its reference to groups that have been discriminated against. It provides a clear example of the way in which the legal framework established by Justice Powell's opinion in *Bakke* channeled the way we thought and spoke about university admissions.

The sentence in question identifies African Americans, Hispanics, and Native Americans as three groups that share two properties: *(a)* they were historically discriminated against, and *(b)* today they would not be present at the Law School in meaningful numbers without some conscious attention in the admissions process. It is important to appreciate that, under the logic of the admissions policy, those two properties were not thought sufficient, in and of themselves, to establish a basis for the use of affirmative action. Affirmative action was not predicated upon a desire to make up for historic discrimination, nor by a desire to maintain a numerical balance among the races of attending students. Rather, the fact of historic discrimination was significant only because it is part of what makes racial diversity a pedagogically meaningful kind of diversity within a law school (unlike, for example, diversity of middle initials). That is why the last sentence of the paragraph identifies students from these groups as being "particularly likely to have experiences and perspectives of special importance to our mission." Similarly, the fact that meaningful numbers of minority students could not be enrolled without affirmative action was not significant for its own sake, nor did it matter whether historic discrimination was the cause of any group's current underrepresentation. Under the policy, all that mattered was that without affirmative action pedagogically meaningful diversity could not be achieved.

Our admissions policy was adopted by the full faculty in 1992. In 1997, the Center for Individual Rights (CIR) filed a lawsuit on behalf of Barbara Grutter, challenging the constitutionality of that policy.

The day after the lawsuit was filed, I wrote a letter to many of

our most important and loyal graduates, setting out the position we intended to follow in the litigation. In the portion of the letter discussing the merits of our position, I wrote:

> As to CIR's legal argument, I am confident that our admissions policy is constitutional. Justice Powell's opinion in *Regents of the University of California* v. *Bakke* affirms that the Fourteenth Amendment does not bar universities from choosing, in the exercise of their sound educational discretion, to adopt admissions policies like ours. I believe that the Supreme Court should not, and will not, use this lawsuit to change the law and eliminate universities' authority to decide whether to make appropriate use of racial diversity as one of many factors in admissions.
>
> As to how that authority is exercised, I believe that our admissions policy . . . helps us to offer the best possible educational environment. *The Law School strives to cultivate in our students the ability to understand an issue from many perspectives.* Students develop this ability through their interactions with the faculty and with one another, inside and outside the classroom.
>
> Race matters in American society, but it is not all that matters. Americans of different races have different experiences that predictably lead them to bring different insights to the study of legal issues as diverse as property law, contract law, criminal justice, social welfare policy, civil rights law, voting rights law, and the First Amendment. At the same time, racial background does not preordain one's views. *A diverse student body allows students to appreciate this complex but important social reality.*
>
> Racial diversity is one of many forms of diversity that we value, and one of many factors in our admissions decisions. Our admissions office does not use quotas; the percentage of students of different races varies noticeably from year to year. And we consider diversity within the larger context of admitting only students whom we expect to become outstanding lawyers.
>
> We believe that the judgment we exercise in admissions is affirmed by the quality of the intellectual experience that our students enjoy, and by the achievements and contributions that

our graduates have made to our society after leaving Ann Arbor. Law School graduates of all races have distinguished themselves as partners in major law firms, holders of federal and state elective office, judges and justices, and senior business executives.

We expect to prevail in this litigation. If we were not to prevail, the lesson from Texas and California is that we would witness a dramatic reduction in the number of African American and Latino students, well qualified for the study and practice of law, who are enrolled in the nation's top law schools. *Such an outcome would be significantly detrimental to the quality of education that we provide.* (Emphasis added)

In hindsight, I find this letter interesting both for what it did and for what it did not do. It tracked closely the terms of the admissions policy itself. It explained the educational goal of legal education (helping students to see problems from multiple perspectives) and the way diversity within the student body promoted that goal. But the letter did not acknowledge the societal cost that follows from any departure from strict color blindness. It did not use the general vocabulary of integration to describe the value that justifies that departure in this case. And it did not explain why a rigidly color-blind admissions policy could not produce a meaningfully integrated entering class.

During the following eighteen months, I was constantly working on the case. The process of discovery was lengthy, involving the production of documents pertaining to our admissions process as well as depositions. I met with newspaper editors to discuss our position. And I had countless conversations with concerned alumni-graduates who loved the Law School but who needed reassurance that we were doing the right thing.

Throughout those conversations, I was impressed with the powerful feelings of ambivalence that many people feel about affirmative action. Not surprisingly, it sometimes triggered very personal fears that they or their children might not be able to enjoy as many life opportunities as they would like. But even when the issue was not felt as a personal issue, many of the people I spoke with felt deeply torn. Using race as a category felt problematic and dangerous. But failing to do so in these circumstances felt just as bad, or worse. I came to believe that it was important for us to speak directly of the conflict between the two attractive ideals of color blindness and integration.

In April 1999, I began to try out such an approach in a speech at a gathering about racial unity where I knew most of the audience supported our position in the litigation. As I prepared to address that audience, I recognized clearly that Justice Powell's academic discussion of diversity provided only a partial explanation for why affirmative action remains necessary. I therefore decided to invoke affirmative action's role in a larger project of integration:

In the end, we will prevail only if we persuade our adversaries of a fundamental but painful fact about America. And that is, in this country, racial integration does not happen by accident. . . .

[O]ur adversaries say that if the Law School ran a colorblind admissions process, most of those 25 seats [occupied by African Americans within a total class of 339] might have gone to white people. That might not have made a difference for 1000 disappointed applicants. But maybe it would have for 15.

And that is precisely my point.

300 years of chattel slavery and 100 years of *de jure* segregation left our country enfeebled. The changes in our legal order that were brought about in 1954 and 1964 were not enough to make that history irrelevant. Not in five years, not in twenty-five years, not in forty-five years.

At the end of the millennium, racial integration in America still does not happen by accident.

Housing in America is hypersegregated by race. According to historian Thomas Sugrue, who is going to testify as an expert in our lawsuit, Detroit is more segregated in 1990 than it was in 1960.

Wealth, opportunity, education, and preparation for law school are not distributed colorblind in America in 1999.

And so we have seen in Texas and California that if a school like ours is prohibited from placing a positive value on having a racially integrated student body, it will not be integrated.

Interestingly, I did not feel comfortable stopping there. After making points that were not part of the "script" furnished by Justice Powell's opinion in *Bakke*, I returned to that script to explain exactly how our admissions process operated:

The CIR lawyers argue that we should not worry about that. That we should fill in our class according to students' "numbers": their undergraduate grade point average and their LSAT test score.

We rely on undergraduate grade point averages and test scores. They do a respectable job of predicting how well someone will do in law school.

But that is not all we rely on.

We look at whether applicants took hard or easy courses. We look at whether they took more demanding or less demanding subjects. We look at whether they attended more competitive or less competitive schools.

We look at how well they write essays. We look at what their professors say about them in letters of recommendation.

And we think about what they will add to the class. We think about what they will add to the profession. We think about what they will add to society.

Because we don't have enough seats for everyone who might be able to do the work. We have to allocate them.

And part of how we allocate them is to promote diversity within our school. Because it's easier to learn how to be a good lawyer if you are interacting with people who are different from yourself. Everyone who attends our law school is better off if we are diverse.

And so we look for diversity of talents. Diversity of experiences. Diversity of undergraduate majors. Diversity of state and city and urban/rural background. And we look for diversity of race.

Then, by way of conclusion, I attempted to draw the two aspects of the speech—the discussion of integration and the discussion of diversity—together into a unified whole. In so doing, I wanted to remind my audience that, in using affirmative action, we were compromising an ideal of color blindness that was important to us as well:

If we did not consider race, we would not be an integrated and diverse school. Racial integration does not happen by accident.

Our adversaries say that it is OK for us to seek diversity in these other dimensions. It is OK for us to consider these features of the individuals who apply for admission. They just want us to slice off one attribute. They want us to try to slice off people's race, and consider them as raceless beings.

And our adversaries are surely right to remind us that, in the long sweep of history, race has been used in pernicious ways. And there is a cost to relying on that category, even though we are doing so for positive reasons. If racial integration could happen by accident, we would prefer not to rely on racial categories in our admissions process. If there were another path to diversity, we would take it.

Maybe some day there will be. Maybe some day white children and black children will really grow up together, in the same neighborhoods, on the same blocks, at the same schools. I hope that our adversaries will work with us to hasten that day.

But that day is not yet here. And pretending that it has arrived will not make it so. Racial integration does not happen by accident. It only happens when people act, affirmatively, to bring it about.

The trial in our case took place in the winter of 2001. That summer, I was asked to write an op-ed as part of a pro-and-con exchange in a journal of higher education called *Matrix*. By that time I had grown accustomed to highlighting the attractions of both color blindness and integration. In that particular op-ed piece, I chose to do so at the very beginning, using the vocabulary of cognitive dissonance.

The psychological literature on cognitive dissonance is familiar and occasionally startling. Experimental subjects who discover an inconsistency between two beliefs will feel tension. They will sometimes alter those beliefs, disregarding evidence if necessary, to relieve that tension.

The debate about affirmative action triggers cognitive dissonance for many people, forcing them to confront an inconsistency between the following beliefs:

- The very finest institutions of higher education should have more than token levels of racial integration.
- The very finest institutions of higher education should make admissions decisions in a rigidly colorblind manner.

Tension arises because today, at the start of the twenty-first century in the United States of America, it is not possible to achieve more than token levels of racial integration at the very finest institutions of higher education by making admissions decisions in a rigidly color-blind manner.

Why is that? One among the many important reasons is that people of different races still tend to grow up in separate worlds. For hundreds of years, American culture and often American law required children of different races to live separately; only during the past forty years has integration been legally permissible everywhere. Moreover, during the past four decades behavioral change has been slow. Ours is not yet a society where integration happens accidentally.

Nor can we yet say that opportunity is distributed in a colorblind manner. It is not yet true that newborns of all races can be expected to receive equal investments in their preschool, elementary, and secondary education. It therefore should not surprise us that the applicant pool at the highest levels of academic competition is not as diverse as the census shows our nation to be.

It is natural to wish that things were different. To wish that we could be colorblind and integrated, if only universities would try harder, or be more creative, or . . . But if it were possible, we would have done those things long ago. In truth teachers and admissions officers and regents do not like the choices that reality imposes any more than ordinary citizens or judges do.

And so we must choose: Integration or Colorblindness.

In the middle portion of the article, I returned to a defense of the manner in which our policy pursued integration, using the parameters established by Justice Powell's opinion in *Bakke*. I tried to be more explicit than I had been before about the precise link between *legal* education and classroom diversity:

By studying law in an integrated environment, our students are better prepared to practice law, to enact laws, and to interpret laws in an integrated society. An outstanding lawyer has an exceptionally well-tuned capacity to engage sympathetically with arguments that are opposed to his or her own beliefs. At the very best law schools, we nurture that capacity. Each day we require students to interact with one another, and to come to understand why—even though they are all extraordinarily bright and articulate—they do not all see the world in the same way. Over the course of three years, they begin to internalize each other's perspectives, so that they become accustomed to holding several inconsistent perspectives on an issue in their minds at the same time.

At this point in the public debate about the lawsuit, our critics had begun to emphasize one seeming paradox about a defense of affirmative action that stressed the pedagogic benefits of diversity. How could we be confident that affirmative action would promote more varied perspectives in the classroom without assuming that a person's race dictated his or her beliefs? Were we not relying on the very stereotypes that we were hoping to break down? At the end of the *Matrix* article, I addressed that concern directly:

> In America today, an individual's race has an important impact on his or her life experiences. It does not necessarily determine that person's ideology or ultimate position on any given policy question. But it is likely to inform the distinctive voice that each of us uses to describe the world we observe. For that reason, a racially diverse classroom tends to offer distinctive benefits for the study of law that are much less likely to be experienced in a more homogeneous classroom.
>
> My experience as a teacher tells me that those benefits are invaluable. And yet I do not mean to suggest that there are no costs to choosing integration over colorblindness. I believe we should all hope for the day when we no longer need to make that choice. But until that day dawns, I also believe we must continue to act, affirmatively, to promote the kind of integrated educational environments through which students are prepared to become sophisticated actors in a diverse, complex society.

As the litigation wound its way through the courts, it came to acquire ever greater symbolic significance in the public eye. At each stage—during the trial in the district court, after the district court ruled against us, and especially after the court of appeals ruled in our favor—it became more and more evident that this would be the case in which the Supreme Court revisited *Bakke*. Along with that progression came an escalation of the rhetoric about the importance of the case.

Perhaps not surprisingly, critics of our policy took to describing it (and us) in exaggerated terms. They mischaracterized it as a "quota" system, and we were called everything from "nuts" to "racists." Just as distressingly, however, *supporters* of our policy also began to exaggerate its significance in the history of racial progress in America.

When, in April 2003, the Mexican American Legal Defense and Educational Fund invited me to be the keynote speaker at its annual awards dinner in Chicago, I had the opportunity to incorporate all of the themes that we had developed over five years of litigation into a single address. I thought it important to begin by warning against the dangers of being excessively grandiose about the case and casting affirmative action in higher education as a significant element in the struggle to right past wrongs. Affirmative action as it is practiced in higher education is not an effort to redress history's injustices. It is at most a pragmatic effort by today's universities to reflect contemporary values and commitments. Integration is a motivating ideal, but it is limited by and balanced against other ideals:

> It has been suggested that I helped to draft a policy that constitutes an important step in the fight for racial justice in America. And in all humility and in all gratitude to those who have said such things, I want to say that such praise is not appropriate and is potentially dangerous. . . . [O]ur admissions policy is not about corrective action, either in its design or in its effect. It is not about racial justice in that sense. . . . No. Our admissions policy resonates with a very different mix of values. It is individualistic. It is meritocratic. It is self-interested. It is, at its core, pragmatic.
>
> Our admissions policy demands that no applicant, of any race, be offered admission unless he or she has the ability to suc-

ceed in an intellectual endeavor that is as demanding as one can find anywhere in higher education. It doesn't matter how much injustice an applicant has experienced in the course of a lifetime. If she can't cut it in our classroom—not just some hypothetical classroom, but our classroom—then she will not be admitted.

I reviewed the by-now-familiar structure of our admissions policy, and discussed the limited role that a concern for racial integration plays within it.

[O]ur interest in having a critical mass of students from different minority groups can be, and has been, attacked as a timid one. For it is considered in context. It is balanced in the case of individual applicant files against other candidates' potential contributions to the collective competence of the class. And so we have never in fact had a critical mass of Native Americans in our class. Even though we reject a majority of Native American applicants every year, just as we reject a majority of applicants of all races every year. And the number of African Americans and Latinos in any given class has swung wildly up and down from year to year, depending on the applicant pool.

Only then did I turn directly to the strongest arguments that were being leveled by our critics. I tried to frame those concerns forcefully and sympathetically, and to ground our responses in a set of widely shared ideals.

So why is CIR so angry with us? Why is it OK for us to take into account whether someone is the child of an alumnus, but not whether the class has a meaningful degree of racial integration? Why is it OK for us to consider the contribution that an applicant's experience traveling the world might make to collective competence, but not for us to consider the contribution racial diversity might make to collective competence?

To our critics, the point is that race is different. To our critics, the fundamental evil of American history has been race-consciousness as opposed to colorblindness. To our critics, the society as a whole is entirely too race-conscious, and it is our special duty as a public institution to set the right example. If the University of Michigan Law School leads the way to rigid, unflinching colorblindness, say our critics, then the rest of the world will follow. If we fail to set a good example, then our society will continue to wallow in racism.

Now I understand this argument. I get the point. I respect the legitimacy of a colorblind ideal.

Having framed this argument and having conceded its force, I then offered two responses. The first questioned the extent to which university admissions policies affect the overall degree of race consciousness in our society:

[T]he unflinching colorblindness argument reflects a kind of utopian wishful thinking that has no connection with the real world. Would rigid colorblindness in admissions to the University of Michigan Law School really hasten the arrival of a general, society-wide colorblindness? Does the society as a whole really care that much about how we run our admissions process?

We're really not that influential. If tomorrow all the universities in America were to announce, with tremendous fanfare, that we will henceforth be rigidly colorblind, I venture to say that we would inspire no change in the level of race consciousness in society. Affirmative action did not create race consciousness and it is not the linchpin that sustains it. It merely responds to a phenomenon that is much larger than we are.

My second response was to invoke the need to balance our commitment to color blindness with our commitment to integration:

[T]he unflinching colorblindness argument . . . depends upon a naïve and simple vision of the world, in which we have only one goal. But that is not true. Our world is difficult and complex. We have many goals. One of them may be colorblindness. But surely a second goal is integration.

How many newspaper stories have we seen over the past decade, expressing a sense of despair at how slow the progress towards integration has been? How many books have been written lamenting the continuing levels of residential segregation in this country, the hesitancy of people to reach out and form friendships across the color line?

Of course, the reason for the tone of despair is that this really is an ideal that we treasure. We really do know that our nation must continue to integrate if we are to prosper in a global economy. And even though progress has been slow, it has also been steady. We are a more integrated society today than we were in 1964. Indeed, even our harshest critics, people like Stephan and Abigail Thernstrom, and Ward Connerly, have praised the ideal of integration.

At this point in my talk, I felt it necessary to address an argument that our critics had begun to advance aggressively in 2002 and 2003. When people experience cognitive dissonance, it is normal for them to try to find ways to resolve the tension without abandoning either of their competing allegiances. In the affirmative action debate, that meant trying to find a way to believe that one could have both color blindness and integration. If that were so, one could oppose affirmative action without opposing integration.

The mechanism that was suggested at the end of the litigation was the so-called percentage plan, under which a university would commit to admit all applicants whose high school grades put them within the top 10 percent of their own high school class. No such mechanism had ever been attempted at the level of graduate or professional schools. And in the undergraduate programs where it had been attempted (most notably Texas and Florida), the schools had used race-conscious mechanisms to design supplementary programs in order to pursue integration. CIR itself had been critical of those programs, and several scholarly analyses had shown them to be ineffectual. Nonetheless, the desire to find a way around choosing between color blindness and integration was so powerful that the solicitor general had filed an amicus brief suggesting that percentage plans made affirmative action unnecessary.

I therefore spent several minutes trying to suggest that this really is an issue without easy answers, and that progress is not to be found by attempting to assign blame for the predicament in which we find ourselves:

> [H]ere is the simple, unvarnished truth. Today, in the year 2003, in the United States of America, one cannot have a colorblind admissions policy at the most selective American law schools and also have integration. To insist on rigid, unflinching colorblindness is to insist on the absence of any meaningful degree of integration at these schools.
>
> Let me be entirely clear about this. This is not the fault of the law schools. It's not as though law schools could have both colorblindness and integration by trying harder, by tweaking their admissions policies this way or that way to place more weight on socioeconomic disadvantage, or by doing a little more recruiting and outreach.
>
> Remember where we live today. We live in a country with a terrible history of racial oppression. Where the disparities in wealth by race are enormous. Where children of all races do not sit side by side in school together. Where the differences in quality of K–12 education are well documented.
>
> How can it be a surprise that, at the end of 16 years of education, rigid and unflinching colorblindness by a graduate school fails to produce integration?
>
> At the University of Michigan Law School, we choose to recognize the pedagogic value of integration. We choose a policy that is grounded in the pragmatic realities of American society today. We recognize that if we are to continue to enjoy the societal benefits that come when the nation's most talented future lawyers study in racially integrated law schools, we must act

affirmatively to acknowledge those benefits. We understand that if we foster integration today, we are more likely to reach a colorblind society in the future. But if we insist on rigid, unflinching colorblindness today, our society will become less integrated, not more.

Our approach has been pragmatic, grounded in the desire to graduate a class of students that has the highest degree of collective competence, given the world we actually live in today. If we could produce a class with the same level of collective competence using a colorblind admissions policy, we would do it today. We can't, and so we engage in affirmative action.

The Supreme Court's decision in *Grutter v. Bollinger* completes an important chapter in public discussion of affirmative action. In many ways, it is appropriately perceived as a direct heir to Justice Powell's opinion in *Bakke,* a reaffirmation of the principles already laid down. But in important ways *Grutter* was a stunning contrast to its predecessor.

To begin with, the Court showed none of the fracturing that had plagued the *Bakke* precedent. A five-justice majority of the Court signed a single opinion. Quasi-metaphysical debates about what constituted the "narrowest" opinion in a case could (thankfully) be diverted to other areas of the law from affirmative action in university admissions.

The consensus extended beyond the majority opinion as well. In a separate opinion, Justice Kennedy seemed to agree that the pursuit of racial diversity could constitute a compelling interest in a university admissions process; his dissent was limited to expressing his belief that the Law School's policy was not "narrowly tailored" to promote that interest. And Chief Justice Rehnquist was silent on the compelling interest question, limiting his dissent to whether the Law School's admissions process was narrowly tailored to promote that interest.

The most important elements of *Grutter,* however, are to be found in the majority opinion by Justice O'Connor. I will emphasize two of those elements.

The first concerns Justice O'Connor's crisp, lucid discussion of what it means to say that under our Constitution, the use of race as a category triggers "strict scrutiny." She wrote:

We are a "free people whose institutions are founded upon the doctrine of equality." It follows from that principle that "government may treat people differently because of their race only for the most compelling reasons."

We have held that all racial classifications imposed by government "must be analyzed by a reviewing court under strict scrutiny." This means that such classifications are constitutional only if they are narrowly tailored to further compelling governmental interests. "Absent searching judicial inquiry into the justification for such race-based measures," we have no way to determine what "classifications are 'benign' or 'remedial' and what classifications are in fact motivated by illegitimate notions of racial inferiority or simple racial politics." We apply strict scrutiny to all racial classifications to "'smoke out' illegitimate uses of race by assuring that [government] is pursuing a goal important enough to warrant use of a highly suspect tool."

Strict scrutiny is not "strict in theory, but fatal in fact." Although all governmental uses of race are subject to strict scrutiny, not all are invalidated by it. *As we have explained, "whenever the government treats any person unequally because of his or her race, that person has suffered an injury that falls squarely within the language and spirit of the Constitution's guarantee of equal protection." But that observation "says nothing about the ultimate validity of any particular law; that determination is the job of the court applying strict scrutiny."* When race-based action is necessary to further a compelling governmental interest, such action does not violate the constitutional guarantee of equal protection so long as the narrow-tailoring requirement is also satisfied.

Context matters when reviewing race-based governmental

action under the Equal Protection Clause. In Adarand Constructors, Inc. v. Pea, we made clear that strict scrutiny must take "'relevant differences' into account." Indeed, as we explained, that is its "fundamental purpose." Not every decision influenced by race is equally objectionable and strict scrutiny is designed to provide *a framework for carefully examining the importance and the sincerity of the reasons advanced* by the governmental decisionmaker for the use of race in that particular context. (*Grutter* v. *Bollinger,* 123 S.Ct. 2325, 2337–38; emphasis added and citations to prior cases omitted)

The elements in this passage that I have emphasized are significant for their sensitivity to the close balance of competing values implicated in the case. Before entering into the close analysis of compelling interests and narrow tailoring that the Fourteenth Amendment requires, the opinion lays two important items of groundwork. First, it acknowledges that all uses of race are injurious. Rather than leaping directly to an explanation of why the policy in question is legally valid, the opinion does the important work of saying that the policy employs a tool that causes real collateral damage, but is, *nevertheless,* lawful. Second, in framing the type of judicial review that such an injurious tool requires, the opinion affirms that a court must evaluate not only the importance of the justification proffered for a government's use of race as a category, but also its *sincerity.* The difficult emotional context that underlies contemporary American discussions of race can tempt policymakers as well as private citizens toward expedient but insincere overstatement. Justice O'Connor's opinion for the majority reminds us that, where government action is concerned, such overstatement is not constitutionally acceptable.

The majority opinion then turns to a discussion of whether the Law School's pedagogic interest in having a racially diverse student body is constitutionally "compelling." The bulk of that discussion consisted of three points. First, the Court reaffirms the constitutional basis for showing some (but by no means absolute) deference to the academic judgment of universities. "We have long recognized that, given the important purpose of public education and the expansive freedoms of speech and thought associated with the university environment, universities occupy a special niche in our constitutional tradition" (*Grutter,* 2339). Quoting Justice Powell's opinion in *Bakke,* the majority reaffirms that

> by claiming "the right to select those students who will contribute the most to the 'robust exchange of ideas,'" a university "seek[s] to achieve a goal that is of paramount importance in the fulfillment of its mission." Our conclusion that the Law School has a compelling interest in a diverse student body is informed by our view that attaining a diverse student body is at the heart of the Law School's proper institutional mission, and that "good faith" on the part of a university is "presumed" absent "a showing to the contrary." (*Grutter,* 2339; citations omitted)

Second, the majority speaks approvingly, in its own voice, of the broad array of evidence that had been presented in support of that educational judgment:

> These benefits are substantial. As the District Court emphasized, the Law School's admissions policy promotes "cross-racial understanding," helps to break down racial stereotypes, and "enables [students] to better understand persons of different races." These benefits are "important and laudable," because "classroom discussion is livelier, more spirited, and simply more enlightening and interesting" when the students have "the greatest possible variety of backgrounds."
>
> The Law School's claim of a compelling interest is further bolstered by its amici, who point to the educational benefits that flow from student body diversity. In addition to the expert studies and reports entered into evidence at trial, numerous studies show that student body diversity promotes learning outcomes,

and "better prepares students for an increasingly diverse work-force and society, and better prepares them as professionals." Brief for American Educational Research Association et al. as Amici Curiae 3; see, e.g., W. Bowen & D. Bok, *The Shape of the River* (1998); *Diversity Challenged: Evidence on the Impact of Affirmative Action* (G. Orfield & M. Kurlaender eds. 2001); *Compelling Interest: Examining the Evidence on Racial Dynamics in Colleges and Universities* (M. Chang, D. Witt, J. Jones, & K. Hakuta eds. 2003).

These benefits are not theoretical but real, as major American businesses have made clear that the skills needed in today's increasingly global marketplace can only be developed through exposure to widely diverse people, cultures, ideas, and view-points. Brief for 3M et al. as Amici Curiae 5; Brief for General Motors Corp. as Amicus Curiae 3–4. What is more, high-rank-ing retired officers and civilian leaders of the United States mili-tary assert that, "[b]ased on [their] decades of experience," a "highly qualified, racially diverse officer corps . . . is essential to the military's ability to fulfill its principle mission to provide national security." Brief for Julius W. Becton, Jr. et al. as Amici Curiae 27. The primary sources for the Nation's officer corps are the service academies and the Reserve Officers Training Corps (ROTC), the latter comprising students already admitted to participating colleges and universities. Id., at 5. At present, "the military cannot achieve an officer corps that is *both* highly qualified *and* racially diverse unless the service academies and the ROTC used limited race-conscious recruiting and admissions policies." Ibid. (emphasis in original). To fulfill its mission, the military "must be selective in admissions for training and educa-tion for the officer corps, *and* it must train and educate a highly qualified, racially diverse officer corps in a racially diverse set-ting." Id., at 29 (emphasis in original). We agree that "[i]t requires only a small step from this analysis to conclude that our country's other most selective institutions must remain both diverse and selective." Ibid. (*Grutter,* 2339–40)

These first two points in the majority's discussion of a university's interest in diversity are well crafted but unsurprising. They closely track Justice Powell's discussion in *Bakke*, broadening and deepening it to reflect the substantial body of experience that universities accumulated between 1978 and 2003. The third point, however, is surprising. Borrowing language from a government brief that had asked the Court to strike down the Law School's policy, the majority instead used the government's argument to extend the constitutional understanding of diversity to incorporate not only a *pedagogic* interest but also an interest in *democratic legitimacy:*

We have repeatedly acknowledged the overriding importance of preparing students for work and citizenship, describing education as pivotal to "sustaining our political and cultural heritage" with a fundamental role in maintaining the fabric of society. This Court has long recognized that "education . . . is the very foundation of good citizenship." For this reason, the diffusion of knowledge and opportunity through public institutions of higher education must be *accessible* to all individuals regardless of race or ethnicity. The United States, as amicus curiae, affirms that "[e]nsuring that public institutions are *open and available* to all segments of American society, including people of all races and ethnicities, represents a paramount government objective." Brief for United States as Amicus Curiae 13. And, "[n]owhere is the importance of such openness more acute than in the context of higher education." Ibid. *Effective participation* by members of all racial and ethnic groups in the civic life of our Nation is essential if the dream of one Nation, indivisible, is to be realized.

Moreover, universities, and in particular, law schools, represent the training ground for a large number of our Nation's leaders. Individuals with law degrees occupy roughly half the state governorships, more than half the seats in the United States Senate, and more than a third of the seats in the United States House of Representatives. See Brief for Association of American Law

Schools as Amicus Curiae 5–6. The pattern is even more striking when it comes to highly selective law schools. A handful of these schools accounts for 25 of the 100 United States Senators, 74 United States Courts of Appeals judges, and nearly 200 of the more than 600 United States District Court judges. Id., at 6.

In order to cultivate a set of leaders with legitimacy in the eyes of the citizenry, it is necessary that the path to leadership be visibly open to talented and qualified individuals of every race and ethnicity. All members of our heterogeneous society must have confidence in the openness and integrity of the educational institutions that provide this training. As we have recognized, law schools "cannot be effective in isolation from the individuals and institutions with which the law interacts." Access to legal education (and thus the legal profession) must be inclusive of talented and qualified individuals of every race and ethnicity, so that all members of our heterogeneous society may participate in the educational institutions that provide the training and education necessary to succeed in America. (*Grutter,* 2340–41; emphasis added, citations to prior cases omitted)

Notice the significance of this discussion. The Court is not speaking about the way in which students of all races become better educated by studying in diverse environments. That was the second point. Rather, the Court is speaking here about the importance to our society of having elite educational institutions be *visibly integrated.*

Throughout this essay, I have stressed the importance of acknowledging that affirmative action is a pragmatic compromise between an appropriate preference for color blindness and an appropriate preference for integration. The majority opinion in *Grutter* resituates our understanding of why a preference for integration is appropriate in the context of higher education. Under *Bakke,* universities were authorized to think about racial integration only to the extent it has immediate implications for professors' teaching and students' learning. Under *Grutter,* universities may consider the fact that, if they lack meaningful levels of integration, others may lack "confidence in the[ir] openness and integrity." Universities, especially public universities, may consider their own missions as entailing more than simply the nourishment of student brains and character. They may understand themselves as important institutional actors in the sustenance of an American society that is open to all, in which any young child may find reason to hope that he or she might have access to the opportunities that this nation offers, regardless of his or her parents' race, religion, or wealth.[2]

There might seem to be an element of paradox in the fact that Justice Powell's narrower vision of diversity did not appear to command the same breadth of support on the Court in 1978 as Justice O'Connor's broader vision did in 2003. After all, no other justice joined the portion of Justice Powell's opinion in which he found universities' interest in pedagogic diversity to be "compelling." In contrast, four other justices joined the portion of Justice O'Connor's opinion in which she found universities' interest in diversity to be compelling both for pedagogic reasons and for reasons of democratic legitimacy. Yet during the intervening quarter century, most Americans seem to have become less supportive of affirmative action rather than more.

One way to resolve that paradox would be to say that it is illusory. In *Bakke* four other justices had joined Justice Brennan's opinion, and Justice Brennan's analysis had been equally supportive of affirmative action. In a footnote he had seemed to endorse the same Harvard undergraduate admissions policy that Justice Powell had endorsed. Indeed, Justice Brennan had been willing to uphold the Davis quota policy that Justice Powell had not been able to tolerate.

Yet while this approach to resolving the paradox will satisfy many, it will not be satisfactory to all. During the years between

Bakke and *Grutter,* some commentators and some courts were not willing to infer that the four justices who joined the Brennan opinion had implicitly accepted Justice Powell's diversity analysis. They argued that the Brennan group had found a path to accepting affirmative action that was not broader than Justice Powell's, only different.

And whether or not one accepts this approach, it might still remain a matter of curiosity why, in a case that seemed to cry out for a decision on the narrowest grounds possible, even a single justice would have been interested in moving from an endorsement of affirmative action based on a narrow understanding of diversity to an endorsement of affirmative action that is based upon a broader understanding of diversity. I believe that the key here is to appreciate that, by relying on a *broader* conception of diversity, the *Grutter* analysis allowed the Court to invoke a *narrower* category of exceptions to color blindness than Justice Powell deployed in *Bakke.*

Under Justice Powell's analysis, the Fourteenth Amendment's presumptive requirement of color blindness could be deemed satisfied whenever a public university could show that a departure from color blindness was necessary to achieve a pedagogic goal. That was a conclusion that many had long found troublesome. No feature of our national history had led to more strife than its centuries of oppression and exclusion on the basis of race. How could something so parochial as a desire to provide better instruction for students be sufficient to warrant the use of a category so fraught with danger? After all, hadn't some of our most shameful historic practices been undertaken under the pretense that they would promote better learning for impressionable young minds?

This concern might be overstated. Pedagogic justifications for Jim Crow exclusion were often pretextual rather than sincere. And even if sincerely held, they often lacked a credible scientific justification. But even with those caveats, it remains true that Justice Powell's understanding of what might make an interest

sufficiently "compelling" to warrant resort to racial classifications has always felt unsatisfying. Racial classifications are the nitroglycerine of American history, volatile and dangerous. Something more than better teaching feels required if they are to be allowed. In order to depart from color blindness, our nation's public institutions should be pursuing the larger national project of integration, a project that is at the core of twenty-first-century America's understanding of itself as democratically legitimate.

Justice Powell's opinion in *Bakke* seemed to say that color blindness may be sacrificed to a university's exercise of autonomy, protected under the First Amendment, that promotes better teaching. Justice O'Connor's opinion in *Grutter* does not go so far. It says only that color blindness may be sacrificed to an exercise of university autonomy that promotes *both* better teaching and a better integrated system of preparing young people for life as adults in a meaningfully integrated working environment.[3]

In their book *Tragic Choices,* Guido Calabresi and Philip Bobbitt considered the problems societies face when they wish to show respect for two incommensurable and inconsistent ideals but are forced to choose between them. They noted some of the strategies that are used, including a seemingly inconsistent pattern of favoring one ideal at one time and the conflicting ideal later. Poignantly, the majority opinion in *Grutter* concludes its analysis with a sentence that signals the Court's hope that such a strategy will be available in this context as well: "We expect that 25 years from now, the use of racial preferences will no longer be necessary to further the interest approved today."

Whether or not we are able to realize that hope, it is clear that the end of the litigation has meant that the national conversation about affirmative action will enter yet another phase. That phase will be shaped in fundamental ways by the Supreme Court's decision to recognize universities' interest in assessing how their admissions policies affect their own legitimacy within our society. The public discussions of the affirmative action litigation brought attention to many features of university admissions that can inspire resentment within the larger society—from early decision processes to preferences for so-called legacies to high tuition rates to reliance on test scores. The interest in ensuring that our important societal institutions hold a measure of democratic legitimacy will likely promote an ongoing discussion of how and whether those features serve universities' institutional missions and meet the needs of our society as a whole.

The litigation about the University of Michigan's admissions policies was ultimately important because it implicated values that shape our national identity. Over the course of the litigation we learned how to speak with greater clarity about those values, and about the tension between them. Whether or not the tension is ever fully resolved, understanding its structure will surely help us to more intelligently confront the challenges ahead.

The Educational Value of Diversity

Patricia Gurin

With Eric L. Dey, Gerald Gurin, and Sylvia Hurtado

I come from a homogeneously white, small town environment and my experience here has really opened my eyes. I consider myself extremely fortunate to have met people during my freshman year who are largely responsible for who I am now. My six best friends could not have been more different from me. Michelle is from Saudi Arabia but is half American, half Thai. Ana is from Madrid, Spain, and is a really strong, feminist woman. Cornelia is African American from Chicago. Suneela is Indian. My roommate, Grace, is Chinese and very religious. Brandi is white but she grew up poor and has beaten the welfare system. She is the most determined person I have ever met. Grace and Suneela are first generation Americans and still have strong ties to their native cultural traditions and language. And, of course, everybody else offered me perspectives I had never thought about or considered before.

I am sure that I could have taken some classes and learned about all of the different things these people have taught me during my years at Michigan. That would have been interesting but because these women became my friends, I got to learn about it *and* experience it. I think that having the experiences is really the only teacher that ever changes how a person thinks about and sees the world. As fantastic as U of M classes can be, I know that they would never have affected me to the extent that these women have.

A WHITE UNDERGRADUATE
writing as a senior at the University of Michigan

This young woman from a small town values her experiences with students from diverse backgrounds because they have changed her world. Her experience reflects the evidence in the social science research provided the courts in the cases testing the University of Michigan's use of race as a factor in admission. This research demonstrates that a racially and ethnically diverse student body has significant educational benefits for all students, nonminority and minority alike.

We presented the courts a social science argument and evidence on the educational value of diversity and were joined by other social scientists in amicus briefs in the cases eventually decided by the Supreme Court. In a five-to-four decision in *Grutter v. Bollinger et al.* (123 S.Ct. 2325, 2337–41), the Court found that

> student body diversity is a compelling state interest that can justify using race in university admissions. . . . Attaining a diverse student body is at the heart of the Law School's proper institutional mission. . . . The Law School's claim is further bolstered by numerous expert studies and reports showing that such diversity promotes learning outcomes and better prepares students for an increasingly diverse workforce, for society, and for the legal profession. Major American businesses have made clear that the skills needed in today's increasingly global marketplace can only be developed through exposure to widely diverse people, cultures, ideas, and viewpoints. High-ranking retired officers and civilian military leaders assert that a highly qualified, racially diverse officer corps is essential to national security. Moreover, because universities, and in particular, law schools, represent the training ground for a large number of the Nation's leaders, Sweatt v. Painter, 339 U.S. 629, 634, the path to leadership must be visibly open to talented and qualified individuals of every race and ethnicity. Thus, the Law School has a compelling interest in attaining a diverse student body. (3–4)

When the University of Michigan was sued by Jennifer Gratz and Patrick Hamacher over its undergraduate admissions procedures and by Barbara Grutter over its Law School admissions procedures, we were asked to determine whether, why, and how diversity has educational benefits. The educational value of diversity was to be a cornerstone of the University of Michigan's arguments, and research evidence was critical. Although the value of diversity had been the rationale for considering race as one of many factors in college admissions ever since the 1978 *Bakke* decision, the arguments offered in other court cases lacked the strong theoretical rationale and empirical evidence needed to link diversity and education. As it turned out, social science research had great importance in the *Grutter* and *Gratz* cases before the Supreme Court.

As social scientists, we addressed three issues: *Does* diversity have educational benefits? *How* and *why* might students benefit from being educated in diverse classrooms and on diverse campuses? We developed a theoretical rationale for the educational value of racial and ethnic diversity, reviewed available evidence, and carried out our own analyses of relevant data sets to test the theory that we offered. In this chapter, we highlight the most important aspects of these materials, including related research that has been conducted since our research was provided to the district court.[1] We also present and respond to questions and criticisms that have been raised about the value of diversity during the legal battle that began in 1997 and was resolved by the Supreme Court in June 2003.

In our expert testimony[2] we emphasized the impact of actual experiences students have with diverse peers (in the classroom and in informal settings on the campus) on two educational outcomes—learning outcomes and democracy outcomes. Thus, from the outset we focused on the broad meaning of diversity: not only how it improves engagement in learning (what Lehman in this volume calls the "pedagogic vision of diversity") but more broadly how it fosters sentiments and skills necessary for citizenship and leadership in a diverse democracy. We argued that experience with diverse peers fosters these educational outcomes, and provided evidence from our own analyses, and the work of other scholars, that supported this argument.

The Educational Rationale

Educators in American higher education have long argued that affirmative action policies are essential to ensure a diverse student body, that such diversity is crucial to creating the best possible educational environment, and that the educational benefits of racial and ethnic diversity on campus are not limited to any one group of students. All students profit from studying in a college or university that includes a significant number of students from backgrounds different from their own.

Institutions of higher education have an obligation, first and foremost, to create the best possible educational environment for those whose lives are likely to be significantly changed during their years on campus. Specific objectives may vary from one institution to another, but all efforts must be directed to ensuring an optimal educational environment for the young people who are at a critical stage of development. At colleges and universities they will complete the foundation of their lives. Universities, furthermore, have an obligation to help build a more truly democratic society, and they have the special strengths needed to do so.

Young people of college age are discovering who they are and what they want to become. A new environment and the presence of others from varied backgrounds may dramatically affect their involvement in learning, their identities in relation to others, the choices they will make for the rest of their lives, and their commitments to citizenship. Identity development in late adolescence and the importance of higher education, especially interaction with peers during the college years, were described in classic works by psychologist Erik Erikson (1946, 1956) and by sociologist Theodore Newcomb (1943) and are now basic to all theories of student development (see Upcraft 1989 for a review of contemporary theories).

Institutions of higher education are especially suited to addressing the developmental tasks of late adolescents, who are defining themselves as mature adults independent from their parents. Residential colleges and universities separate the young person from his or her past. They allow students to experiment with new ideas, new relationships, and new roles. Both undergraduate and graduate years are a time of exploration and possibility, before young people make permanent adult commitments. Most educators recognize that the individuals with whom one is educated may be just as important as where one is educated.

Theories of cognitive growth also emphasize the importance of experiences that contrast with one's past, termed "disequilibrium" by the Swiss psychologist Jean Piaget (1971, 1985). Scholars of cognitive development emphasize the critical role of equality in peer relationships and of multiple perspectives in intellectual and moral development. Children and adolescents can best develop a capacity to understand the ideas and feelings of others—what is called "perspective taking"—and can move to a more advanced stage of moral reasoning when they interact with others from different backgrounds who may hold different perspectives and who are also equals. Both diversity and equality in the relationship are necessary for intellectual and moral development.

The Importance of Diverse Environments

Not all institutions of higher education equally encourage identity formation, cognitive growth, and preparation for citizenship. A homogeneous college environment, for example, that replicates the home community's social life and expectations does not encourage the personal struggle and consciousness of thought that are so important for student development. In contrast, campus environments that foster interaction among students from varied racial and ethnic backgrounds promote the mental and psychological growth that is essential if young people are to move on to fulfilling lives.

It is important to point out that most students have lived in segregated communities before coming to college. About 90 percent of white students and about 50 percent of African American students who entered the University of Michigan in the early 1990s, when our research was conducted, grew up in racially homogeneous neighborhoods and attended racially homogeneous high schools. Only Michigan's Asian American and Latino/a students had much experience with diversity before college, largely because they had attended nearly exclusively white high schools and lived in predominantly white neighborhoods.

In expert testimony submitted on behalf of the university's defense of its admission policies, Thomas Sugrue (1999) dramatically details the racial experiences of applicants from Michigan, New York, Illinois, California, New Jersey, and Ohio, who make up about three-quarters of the university's applicant pool. In those states the typical white student went to public school with no more than 7 percent African American students, and in all states but California with no more than 5.5 percent Latino. (California is an exception in that 21.5 percent of the students in schools attended by typical white students were of Latino origin.) Professor Sugrue also points out that the top four states in degree of black/white school segregation are among these six states with the largest number of applicants to the University of Michigan (Michigan, New York, Illinois, and New Jersey). Segregation is equally dramatic for students of color.

By 1980, 17 of the nation's 20 largest cities had predominantly minority school districts. Most of them are surrounded by overwhelmingly white suburban school districts. As a consequence, University of Michigan demographer Reynolds Farley has shown, these public schools are almost as racially segregated as those which were constitutionally permitted before the 1954 *Brown* decision. (Sugrue 1999, 35)

This segregated precollege background means that many students, white and minority alike, enter college—the University of Michigan and many others—without experience in interacting with others whose backgrounds differ from their own. Consequently, colleges that have made efforts to diversify their student bodies and to institute policies that foster genuine interaction across race and ethnicity provide the first opportunity for many students to learn from others who have different backgrounds and life experiences. They will learn about these differences, and they will also learn about similarities as well. In an environment that is different from their own backgrounds and thus unfamiliar, students are forced to consider new ideas and confront new feelings. It is through diversity on campus that they face change and challenge, the necessary conditions for intellectual growth and for preparation for citizenship in the diverse democracy that America is increasingly becoming.

Several students remarked on their homogeneous backgrounds and how Michigan's diversity has fostered their growth:

> I lived in a black neighborhood for my entire life. I always attended black schools. I do not fault my mother for not providing me with a multicultural background, because that was just how things were. My outlook has definitely broadened here. My assumptions about other cultures have been challenged and I have been stretched in many ways. (An African American woman who grew up in Detroit)

> I grew up in a major California city but I lived and went to school primarily in an Asian American situation. I got a lot of multicultural experience while I was in high school by being part of a city-wide organization that drew from many different cultural groups. Being at U of M is the first time I have been in a

diverse educational place. It was my choice to come here because of its diversity. I wanted to be in a place where diverse people get together, really get together, not just co-exist. (An Asian American male from California)

I am Jewish. When I was little, I thought everybody was Jewish. All I had known was Jewish. All of my friends and what seemed like my whole town was Jewish. It is only recently that I am able to reflect back on the town I grew up in. In my freshman year in high school, I moved from Long Island into the city (Manhattan). That gave me many opportunities. The city has no "supposed to." I could just be me. And I could meet all kinds of people. This is what the U of M is doing for me also. But I have to work at it, to not just fall back into an exclusively Jewish world. (A Jewish woman from New York)

My high school was split between black and white, and a few other minorities. My graduating class was about 250. But even though there was opportunity to know kids from different races, all of my friends were white. Once here, however, I had a big change. Now not all of my friends are white. I have a few really close friends who are African American and Asian American. I have learned so much from all of them. We're a real group. We could be an advertisement for diversity working at Michigan. I would be oh so much more ignorant if I hadn't had this experience. (A white male from a midsize town in Illinois)

Engagement in Learning through Experience with Diverse Peers

So far we have made two arguments: first, that heterogeneous environments are crucial for fostering student growth in late adolescence; second, that most students entering the University of Michigan came from fairly segregated environments. Using research in social psychology from the last twenty years, we will now explain *why* experience with diverse peers fosters active engagement in learning.

A curriculum that deals explicitly with social and cultural diversity, and a learning environment in which students interact frequently with others who differ from themselves in significant ways, affect the *content* of what is learned. Less obvious, however, is the notion that features of the learning environment affect students' *mode of thought,* and that diversity produces more active thinking and can inspire intellectual engagement and motivation.

Many terms are used in social and cognitive psychology to describe two opposing modes of thought: automatic versus nonautomatic; preconscious versus conscious; peripheral versus central; heuristic versus systematic; mindless versus minded; effortless versus effortful; implicit versus explicit; active versus inactive. Whatever the term, research in social psychology has shown that active thinking and engagement in learning cannot be assumed. This research confirms that much apparent thinking and thoughtful action are actually automatic, or what psychologist Ellen Langer (1978) calls *mindless.* To some extent, mindlessness is the result of previous learning that has become so routine that thinking is unnecessary. Instead of thinking through an issue anew, individuals rely on scripts or schemas that operate automatically.

Automatic thinking plays a pervasive role in all aspects of everyday life, in some instances as a necessary strategy for coping with multiple stimuli in a complex environment. Automatic thinking is often evident not only in perceptual processes and in the execution of such skills as driving and typing, but also in evaluation, emotional reactions, determination of goals, and social behavior itself (Bargh 1997). One of our tasks as educators is to interrupt these automatic processes and facilitate active thinking in our students. Higher education needs to find ways to produce the more active, less automatic mode of thinking among students.

In one of the early studies indicating the pervasiveness of automatic thinking, Langer (1978) laid out many positive psychological benefits that occur when people are encouraged to use active, effortful, conscious modes of thought rather than automatic thinking. Conscious, effortful thinking helps people develop new ideas and new ways of processing information, ways that may have been available to them previously but were not often used. In several experimental studies, she showed that such thinking increases alertness and greater mental activity—surely something all college teachers strive for in classrooms.

We know that certain conditions encourage effortful, minded, and conscious modes of thought, for example, novel situations for which people have no script or with which they have no past experience. Active thinking is also promoted in a situation that is not entirely novel but is not entirely familiar either, and thus demands more than their scripts allow people to grasp (Langer 1978). A third situation is one that is discrepant from one's past experiences. In novel, somewhat unfamiliar, and discrepant situations, people have to think about what is going on and struggle to make sense of the environment.

Many people face the demands of novelty, instability, unpredictability, multiplicity, and discrepancy when they take up work or travel in a country with a distinctive and unfamiliar culture, with a language that they do not know and customs and social expectations that they do not understand. They have to pay close attention to new social cues, think deeply about what they perceive, and actively try to understand what is going on.

These conditions are exactly what racial and ethnic diversity provides for students coming to college from racially segregated environments. The informal world where students interact with diverse peers in student organizations, residence halls, and casual social settings and the formal classrooms at Michigan provide the *novelty, instability, discontinuity,* and *discrepancy*[3] that are needed to promote active, conscious, effortful thinking—as evidenced by the experience of another student:

I come from a town in Michigan where everyone was white, middle-class, and generally pretty closed-down to the rest of the world, although we didn't think so. It never touched us, so I never questioned the fact that we were "normal" and everyone else was "other" and "different." Listening to other students in class, especially the African American students from Detroit and other urban areas just blew me away. We live only a few hours away and yet we live in completely separate worlds. Even more shocking was the fact that they knew about "my world" and I knew nothing about theirs. Nor did I think that this was even a problem at first. I realize now that people like me can go through life and not have to see another point of view, that somehow we are protected from it. The beginning for me was when I realized that not everyone shares the same views as I, and that our different cultures have a lot to do with that.

Citizenship and Leadership for a Diverse Democracy

Certainly from the time of the founding of our country, education has been seen as the key to achieving an effective citizenry. Democracy, indeed, is predicated upon an educated citizenry. Thomas Jefferson forcefully argued that citizens are made, not born, and that education was the key to making citizens. Jefferson, however, was talking about education only for citizens. His notion of democracy assumed social homogeneity and common identity rather than social complexity and diversity. Nevertheless, Jefferson is a critical figure in rationalizing the role of higher education in civic preparedness, a project expressed in his role in the founding of the University of Virginia in 1823: "It remained clear to Jefferson to the end of his life that a theory of democracy that is rooted in active participation and continuing consent by each generation of citizens demands a civic pedagogy rooted in the obligation to educate all who would be citizens" (Barber 1998, 169). Like the other great public institutions, the University of Michigan, founded in 1817, had from its beginnings the mission of providing knowledge for the betterment of civil society. The mission of the College of Literature, Sciences, and Arts, inscribed in marble in its central office, has guided the college from its earliest state: "Artes Scientia Veritas—Religion, morality, and knowledge being necessary to good government and the happiness of mankind, schools and the means of education shall forever be encouraged."

If education is the very foundation of democracy, how does diversity foster democracy? The compatibility of diversity and democracy is not self-evident, nor is the implication of diversity for civic unity and disunity a new problem. How to achieve unity, despite or because of difference, has been a central theme in democratic theory ever since the ancient Greeks. In her 1992 book, *Fear of Diversity*, University of Michigan political scientist Arlene Saxonhouse details the debates that took place in ancient Greece about the impact of diversity on capacity for democracy. Plato, Saxonhouse says, envisioned a city-state in which unity and harmony would be based on the shared characteristics of a homogeneous citizenry, a conception of democracy that has prevailed in the United States. Plato's pupil Aristotle, however, advanced a political theory in which unity would be achieved through difference. Saxonhouse writes, "Aristotle embraces diversity as the others had not. . . . The typologies that fill almost every page of Aristotle's *Politics* show him uniting and separating, finding underlying unity and significant differences" (235). He contended that democracy based on such unity would be more likely to thrive than one based on homogeneity. What makes democracy work, according to Aristotle, is equality among citizens who are peers (admittedly only free men at the time, not women and not slaves), but who hold diverse perspectives and whose relationships are governed by freedom and rules of civil discourse. It is discourse over conflict, not unanimity, Aristotle believed, that helps democracy thrive (Pitkin and Shumer 1982).

Common conceptions of democracy in the United States do not

treat difference and conflict as congenial to unity, however. In general, lay understandings of democracy and citizenship take one of two forms: (1) a liberal, individualist conception in which citizens out of self-interest participate through voting for public servants to represent them or through other highly individual ways, and (2) a direct participatory conception, in which people from similar backgrounds who are familiar with each other come together and share a common, overarching identity, as in the New England town meeting, to debate the common good. Both of these conceptions privilege individuals rather than groups, and similarities rather than differences.

The increasingly heterogeneous population in the United States challenges the relevance of these popular conceptions of democracy. Neither is a sufficient model for democracy for the United States today (or for that matter for democracies in the increasingly heterogeneous societies all over the world). What is needed is a multicentric democratic vision. "Neither Rousseau's democratic order as an overarching common identity nor Locke's minimalist conception of a collection of separate self-interests aggregated into a limited state will suffice as a proper vision for the type of democracy necessary today" (Guarasci and Cornwell 1997, 8).

There is little wonder that the United States and its universities specifically are now facing cultural, disciplinary, and political debates over the extent to which democracy can survive with greatly increased heterogeneity and so many group-based claims in the polity. Yet it is clear that an ethnic hierarchy and one-way assimilation, both of which call for the muting of differences and cultural identities, are unlikely to prevail in the future (Fredrickson 1999). "We need a democratic order that can contain the contradiction of difference and connection, self and community, one and many" (Guarasci and Cornwell 1997, 8). It is a vision of democracy in which difference and democracy are mutually compatible.

Several dimensions of preparation for citizenship can be discerned from the theories of Aristotle and Piaget that can make difference and democracy mutually compatible. The conditions deemed important include the presence of diverse others and diverse perspectives; equality among peers; and discussion under rules of civil discourse. In our research we proposed that these conditions foster the orientations that students need to be citizens and leaders in a diverse democracy when they leave college: perspective taking, mutuality and reciprocity, acceptance of conflict as a normal part of life, capacity to perceive differences and commonalities both within and between groups in society, interest in the social world, and citizen participation.

Theoretically, students educated in institutions that include students from varied backgrounds are more motivated and better prepared to be citizens and leaders in an increasingly heterogeneous democracy. However, to be prepared to participate effectively in the U.S. democracy and as global citizens, students need to understand the multiple perspectives inherent in a diverse situation, to appreciate the common values and integrative forces that incorporate differences in the pursuit of the broader common good, and to understand and accept cultural differences that arise in a racially and ethnically diverse society and world.

Summary of the Educational Rationale

In summary, we argue that students' experiences with racial and ethnic diversity have far-ranging and significant educational benefits for both learning and democracy outcomes, and that these benefits extend to all students, nonminorities and minorities alike. Because diversity is crucial for education, universities are obliged to create the best possible educational environments by building a diverse student body, and to use that resource—much as they use other educational resources such as an excellent faculty, infrastructure, or library—to foster learning and civic preparedness. Only in such a setting can students of all racial and ethnic backgrounds acquire the tools needed for a life of engagement in active learning and contribution to a democratic society.

Evidence in Support of the Theoretical Rationale

Racial and ethnic diversity are likely to foster learning and democracy outcomes, but these effects do not happen automatically. Institutions of higher education have to make appropriate use of the racial and ethnic diversity on their campuses. They have to make college classrooms and informal educational settings authentic public places, where students from different backgrounds can take part in conversations and share experiences that help them develop an understanding of the perspectives of other people.

Such learning and understanding are captured in one student's response to a classroom experience at the University of Michigan:

The most helpful aspect of the course was reading the articles from so many different perspectives and then discussing them with students from so many different racial and ethnic groups in class. Living through the heated discussions in class and being asked to participate actually rocked my world and opened some doors. I realized that my past pattern of not talking in class and being invisible was a way of avoiding having to think about or engage in difficult and complex issues. Now that I have engaged and even disagreed with others, it seems like there is no turning back. I'm ready now to wrestle with ideas and multiple perspectives. This change has spilled over into other areas of my life also. I actually am doing much better in my other classes because I am not afraid to think, speak and be challenged intellectually. This finally feels like what college is supposed to be about.

Another student comments about the impact of experience with diversity on his growing commitment to citizenship.

Before coming to Michigan and getting to know so many different kinds of people, and before I took classes specifically on race in America, I never thought of myself as political. I am ashamed to say that I didn't even vote in the last election, even though I was old enough. Now I realize that was because I didn't want to bother about any part of the world outside of my own social circle. Politics was "out there"; I was "in here" in my own little world. Ironically, it was by hearing stories from African American students from Detroit and Latino students from the southwest that opened up my eyes to the limits of always being "in here." I no longer want the walls. I'd rather have a full life. Part of that life is that I do see myself as being a citizen and making a difference in the communities in which I will eventually live.

However powerful such testimony may be, it is not sufficient to compel acceptance of our theoretical rationale for the importance of diversity in the college experience. To determine how engagement in learning and development of democratic sentiments are related to experiences with diversity, as our theoretical rationale says they should be, we reviewed the literature on higher education and undertook three analyses of existing databases: a multi-institutional national study of college students, a study of a cohort of University of Michigan students, and a study of a University of Michigan course on intergroup relations. Because we were able to analyze how diversity influences student learning and democracy outcomes at the national level, the institutional level (focusing on the University of Michigan), and at the level of a classroom in which interaction among students from varied backgrounds was fully integrated with course content, we could take both macroscopic and microscopic looks at how diversity works at various levels. The outcomes we examined conform to the learning and democracy consequences we have proposed.

Our research considered three categories of measures of engagement in learning:

- Growth in active thinking processes that reflect a more complex, less automatic mode of thought
- Intellectual engagement and motivation
- Growth in a broad range of intellectual and academic skills

We focused on four categories of democracy measures:

- Perspective taking, which measures the motivation to understand other people's points of view
- Citizenship engagement, which measures motivation to participate in activities that affect society and the political structure, as well as actual participation in political and community activities during college and in community service in the five years after leaving college
- Racial/cultural engagement, which measures cultural knowledge and awareness, and motivation to participate in activities that promote racial understanding
- Compatibility of differences, which includes the belief that basic values are common across racial and ethnic groups, and the belief that differences are not inevitably divisive to the fabric of society

The Studies: What Did We Do, and How Did We Do It?

To determine how learning and civic preparedness for a diverse democracy are related to students' experiences with diversity, as our theoretical review suggests that they should be, we conducted several statistical analyses of these three sets of data. These systematic analyses were designed to provide scientific insight into the processes by which students are changed by their college experiences. Three characteristics of these analyses should be noted: they are based on data collected over time; they take choices and consequences into account; and they provide both a national and a local University of Michigan perspective.

Data over Time

Growth and development among college students obviously takes place over time. As a result, the most effective research approaches use data collected from the same individuals at more than one time point. This longitudinal approach, in which researchers collect information from students on two or more occasions, allows a systematic analysis of how students develop by comparing data collected from individuals at one time to data collected from these same individuals at later points in time. Moreover, by relating patterns of growth to the educational conditions and activities that students experience between the times the data were collected, we can understand how different experiences promote growth and development among college students.

Taking Choices and Consequences into Account

In studying students over time we recognize that individuals do not make choices randomly, nor do they leave their previous attitudes and experiences at the front door when they enter college. As a result, the choices that students make (and the consequences that these choices have) need to be taken into account in order to make sound judgments about how campus experiences affect students.

For example, we are likely to find that students majoring in mathematics and science have growing interest in science, as compared to those majoring in the humanities. While this may seem to prove that growth in scientific interest is caused by majoring in science, it is important to recognize that those who were drawn into science majors are likely to have been more interested in science when they entered college. In order to make a fair judgment about whether majoring in science or the humanities is differentially related to growth in an interest in science, we need first to take into account the initial differences in interest between these two groups.

Similarly, to study the growth and development of learning and democracy outcomes as related to diversity experiences, it is important to take into account (or control for) differences across individuals in their initial position on measures of learning and democracy, as well as their tendency to be drawn to diversity-related experiences. When we do this, we can be reasonably sure that a positive outcome of diversity experiences does not simply reflect the fact that students who had those experiences were already more positive on that outcome when they entered college.[4]

The Data: National and Local

The databases we used offer two perspectives—one local to Michigan and the other national in scope—that create a comprehensive view of how diversity experiences affect student outcomes. The national data, provided by the Cooperative Institutional Research Program (CIRP) and the UCLA Higher Education Research Institute, were collected from 11,383 students attending 184 colleges and universities. The students entered in 1984, were followed through their senior year in 1989, and were tested again five years later in the postcollege world. The Michigan data were provided by the Michigan Student Study (MSS), which examined 1,582 students on the educational dynamics of diversity on the Michigan campus. The Michigan data came from a series of extensive questionnaires given to all undergraduate students of color and a large, representative sample of white students at the time they entered the University of Michigan in 1990, and again at the end of their first, second, and senior years. We used the entrance and fourth-year data in our studies.

What Do We Mean by Racial/Ethnic Diversity?

Diversity has three meanings. First, there is "structural diversity," represented by the percentage of a student body that is from an ethnic/racial group other than white. Second, there is "classroom diversity," defined as exposure to knowledge about race and ethnicity in formal classrooms. Third, there is "informal interactional diversity," indicated by the extent to which students interact with peers from racial/ethnic backgrounds different from their own. Classroom and informal interactional diversity carry the most important causal role in explaining how racial and ethnic diversity produce educational outcomes for students because they tell us about students' *actual experiences with diversity*. A student may attend a racially/ethnically diverse institution but live a life at college that is nearly exclusively with peers from his/her own racial/ethnic background. What role, then, does structural diversity play in the positive impact of diversity on students?

Structural diversity has two major effects. First, it makes actual experience with diversity possible. Longitudinal studies show that in colleges and universities with greater proportions of racial/ethnic minority students, white students are more likely to socialize and develop friendships with peers of a different race/ethnicity, and discuss racial issues with peers (Chang 1996; Milem and Hakuta 2000; Hurtado, Dey, and Trevino 1994; Antonio 1998). An especially important study—important because it was carried out at a time when affirmative action had become highly politicized—showed that students at 461 colleges and universities were most likely to engage in four kinds of cross-racial interactions (eating together, studying together, dating, and interacting with someone of a different racial/ethnic background) on the most diverse campuses (Chang, Astin, and Kim, 2004). Second, structural diversity increases the range of student viewpoints, and thus fosters intellectual diversity (Chang, Seltzer, and Kim, 2002).

Structural diversity is important, therefore, *because* it enables more students to have actual experience with diverse peers, and because with diversity in backgrounds students are exposed to a broader range of viewpoints based on their different experiences in life. This does *not* imply that all members of an ethnic or racial group think alike, only, that on average, race—just like growing up in a rural or urban environment, in privilege or hardship, in different parts of the country, and so on—is correlated with perspectives on the way society operates. Indeed, there is ample evidence to this effect (Bobo 2001).

We contend, however, that it is classroom and informal interactional diversity that carries the critical causal role in explaining how diversity influences student outcomes. Structural diversity may be thought of as a necessary but not sufficient condition for students to gain educationally from racial/ethnic diversity in higher education. Our work focuses, therefore, on the impact of actual experience with diversity in classes and in the informal campus world.

In the national study, "classroom diversity" was measured by only a single question—enrollment in an ethnic studies class. As a consequence, we found that, while informal interaction with diverse peers had consistent effects for all four groups of students (African American, Asian American, white, Latino/a), classroom diversity had effects on only some outcomes and only for some groups. (See the full presentation of findings in the *Harvard Educational Review,* Gurin et al. 2002.) Therefore, in this chapter experience with diversity in the national study means informal interaction, which was measured by the frequency with which students socialized with a person of a different race, discussed racial issues, or attended cultural awareness workshops over the four years of college.

In the Michigan study, we investigated three kinds of diversity experiences, and for the analyses we carried out for this chapter we brought them together into one measure reflecting overall experience with diversity during the four years of college. (See Gurin et al. 2002 for a presentation of the *separate* effects of the three kinds of diversity experiences.) One kind of diversity experience was in classrooms;[5] it was represented by how much students said they had been exposed in classes to "information/activities devoted to understanding other racial/ethnic groups and inter-racial ethnic relationships," and if they had taken a course during college that had an important impact on their "views of racial/ethnic diversity and multiculturalism." A second kind of diversity experience, informal interaction with diverse peers, included both amount and quality of interaction. Positive quality of interracial/interethnic interactions was represented by the extent to which students said their most frequent cross-racial interactions had involved "meaningful, and honest discussions about race and ethnic relations" and "sharing of personal feelings and problems." Quantity of cross-racial interaction came from the students' assessment of amount of contact they had at Michigan with racial/ethnic groups other than their own. A measure that involved both quality and quantity represented the number of their six best friends at college who were not of their own racial/ethnic group. A third kind of diversity experience measured participation in multicultural campus events and intergroup dialogues. The multicultural campus events were Hispanic/Latino(a) Heritage Month, Native American Month (the annual Pow Wow), Asian American Awareness Week, the Martin Luther King Jr. Symposium, and Black History Month. Intergroup dialogues, offered on the Michigan campus within various courses, involve weekly sessions of structured discussion between an equal number of members (usually seven or eight) from each of two identity groups (Arab/Jewish, Anglo/Latino/a, men/women, African American/white, Native American/Latino/a, and others). The students discuss contentious issues that are relevant to their particular groups.

Learning Outcomes

The analyses we are summarizing here are based on the composite measures of both diversity experiences and of learning outcomes.

What did these analyses of the national and Michigan data tell us about the impact of diversity experiences on learning outcomes? (See Gurin et al. 2002 for the tabular presentation of the effects of the different types of diversity experiences on learning outcomes.)

As we had predicted, the students who had the most diversity experiences in their college years showed the greatest engagement in active thinking processes, self-reported growth in intellectual engagement and motivation, and growth in subjectively assessed intellectual and academic skills. This general conclusion is supported by four major points that can be drawn from analyses conducted for the litigation.

- The analyses reveal a pattern of consistent, positive relationships between learning outcomes and students' experiences with diversity, and these effects apply across students in four ethnic/racial groups (African American, white, Latino(a)[6] and Asian American).
- The results are also consistently positive across multiple learning outcome measures designed to capture students' active thinking processes, intellectual skills and abilities, and motivations for educational progress.
- The results are confirmed in two different studies of the college experience, one that examined effects across 184 institutions (the Cooperative Institutional Research Program national study), and one that focused on the University of Michigan (the Michigan Student Study).
- The results can reasonably be talked about as having demonstrated effects of experience with diversity. (See our discussion above on choices and consequences. No field study in which it is impossible to randomly assign students to high- or low-experience conditions can conclusively demonstrate "effect." However, our procedures go a long way to insure that the results actually come from the experiences students had with classroom and informal interactional diversity, and not primarily from certain kinds of students choosing to have diversity experiences in college.)

In the national study all four groups (white, African American, Asian American, and Latino(a) students) who reported the greatest amount of diversity experience during college were the *most* intellectually engaged at the end of college, after adjusting for how intellectually engaged they were when they entered college. Intellectual engagement was represented by drive to achieve, intellectual self-confidence, interest in attending graduate school, importance placed on writing original works, and creating artistic works. Diversity experience also had positive effects, for all groups of students, on self-reported academic skills, represented by how much they felt they had changed over their college years in general knowledge, analytical/problem solving skills, ability to think critically, writing skills, and foreign-language skills, as well as by increases from freshman to senior year in self-ratings of academic ability, writing ability, and listening ability. Because entrance measures of the three self-ratings of ability were used as statistical controls in assessing the effect of diversity experience, we can be fairly well assured of the conclusion that diversity experience increased these students' sense of their academic competence since entering college.

In the Michigan study, white, African American, and Asian American students who had the greatest amount of experience with diversity during their college years were the *most* intellectually engaged at the end of college. Intellectual engagement was indicated by the students' assessment that they had gained "a broad, intellectual exciting education at Michigan," and their level of satisfaction with the "intellectual quality and challenge of classes."

An example of the meaning of this finding comes from a student who attributes her involvement with ideas and learning to interacting with students with many different kinds of experiences:

I have found in my four years here that I have benefited by being forced to deal with people and cultures that I am unfamiliar with. I am here to learn and I feel my most important learning came from personal experiences—challenges in dealing with

people who are different from me. .... It has given me the opportunity to meet people and work with people who "make waves,"
who talk different from me, who look different from me, who
grew up on the other side of the town, who sometimes don't
even speak English as their first language, who are the first ones
in their family to go to college. The people whom I differ from
the most are the ones I have learned from the most. I got really
turned on to ideas and understanding the world from dealing
with Michigan's diversity.

There was also a significant effect of diversity experience on
active, engaged thinking for all three groups of students. White,
African American, and Asian American students who had the
greatest amount of experience with diversity at Michigan were also
the most motivated for active thinking as fourth-year students,
controlling for their scores on this same measure of active thinking
when they entered college four years before. These results mean
that diversity experience had fostered active thinking over and
beyond student predispositions to think actively about human
behavior when they entered college. Active thinking was measured
by such items as "prefer complex rather than simple explanations
for people's behaviors," "enjoy analyzing the reasons or causes for
people's behaviors," "think about the influence society has on other
people."

A faculty member who teaches courses on language reports how
racial and ethnic diversity in his classroom fostered the students'
awareness of complexity.

The course is about Americanization processes in language, that
all spoken English in the United States had at one point or
another resulted from such processes. To make this vivid for students, I asked them to do a language study of their own background. The diversity in the classroom produced multiple examples of Americanization. In discussing these they also became
aware of the extraordinary complexity there is in ethnicity and

race. One African-American student had a grandfather who was Cherokee. His grandfather had learned English in an Indian boarding school. This student told some of the stories he had heard from his grandfather, who, when married, had become assimilated into the black world. The other students in the class were not prepared for this non-obvious part of this student's identity, and it forced them to see race, ethnicity, and language in much more complex ways. If there hadn't been diversity in this class, the course would not have been as successful. The students learned not only about their own Americanization histories in language but also about the histories of other students from rich diverse ethnicities. It certainly made for a more complex understanding of Americanization, English, and what is "standard" English.

Another faculty member makes a similar point about complexity from a philosophy course on law and philosophy. She describes a student presentation on the validity of campus student organizations organized around lines of race and ethnicity.

The student argued that racial distinctions were harmful but that affiliations along ethnic lines were relatively benign. Therefore, it would be wrong to have a White Students Organization (or, by parallel reasoning, a Black Students Organization), but alright to have an Irish-American Organization. She argued that the latter organization would, as a matter of fact, exclude blacks, but that this exclusion was not racist because the purpose of the organization was not racial exclusion. An African American student in the class objected: "What makes you think I wouldn't be entitled to join the Irish-American Organization? My mother is Irish-American." All of the students were stunned. They learned something about the complexity of race and ethnicity, and the peculiarities of racial definition in America!

One thing that this story illustrates, the professor continues, is the power of knowledge that is gained through personal sharing.

The particular objection to what the student had been saying had not crossed my mind as an instructor, even though I had just been teaching about the one-drop rule (of racial classification in the United States) in lecture. But the error in the student's claims was evident to someone who personally identified as mixed-race. This shows why it is so important to have diverse students in the classroom, and not depend on some abstract discussion among whites only about diversity issues. Whites can have "book" knowledge of some relevant fact but not be able to summon it up when it is needed, because it is not salient to them. The same applies, of course, to members of any race—different sets of facts are salient to them because of their racial identities.

The professor is saying that diversity in the classroom provides the opportunity—when utilized by the faculty—to show that social knowledge requires active exploration of phenomena that do not fit prior conceptions and expectations.

Students also attest to the impact of classroom diversity on their engagement in learning and deeper understanding of multiple assumptions and perspectives.

The major way that diversity has increased my involvement in learning is seeing how many different assumptions people bring to a discussion. It has been fascinating to become aware of different ways of thinking, and often assumptions and ways of thinking go back to the experiences that students had before they came to Michigan.

Students who have grown up in different countries and different cultures in this country are often very inquisitive and ask a lot of questions in class. At least they do when the professor encourages that. When others are active in class, it helps me to become more active also. It becomes a "turned on" environment. Several English literature classes have helped me because they allowed students to talk about the relationship between literature and politics, cultures, and the world. Diverse students who have different life experiences make those discussions really interesting.

Hearing things from students with many different backgrounds and life experiences has taught me to put things in perspective, to explore motives and perspectives, and not just take things at face value. I go beneath what I read and hear now, and diversity is responsible for that. Also I want to learn more. Someone says something that strikes me as novel, that I didn't know anyone thought or had experienced. And I want to get beneath it, to understand it. I have become a whole lot more curious. I was pretty much ready to accept things my community stood for.

The philosophy professor and one of the students point to a crucial condition for classroom diversity to be effective. Professors have to foster open discussion and utilize the potential of student diversity to bring out multiple points of view for classroom diversity to have educational benefits.

The Research of Other Scholars on Learning Outcomes

Evidence supporting the impact of actual experience with diversity on learning outcomes comes from other scholars as well as from the data that we analyzed and from the comments of students attending the University of Michigan. Two major types of studies carried out by other scholars have shown supportive results. First, the vast majority of these studies, like ours, have tied measures of students' experiences with diversity in the classroom and in the broader campus environment to measures of student outcomes. In these studies, evidence for the impact of diversity comes from analysis of the data, not from asking students to assess the effect of diversity themselves. Another important characteristic of this first type of research is that nearly all of these studies are longitudinal in nature, following the same students over time and tying their experiences in college to changes in outcomes across time. The second type of studies, fewer in number, have asked students themselves (or faculty or administrators) to give their subjective assessment of how much experience with diversity has affected student learning.[7] These studies, using different samples and a variety of measures, have shown consistent effects on engagement in learning and thinking.

Relevant to our findings regarding informal interaction, Chang (1999) found that there was the most interracial interaction on campuses with the greatest amount of student racial/ethnic diversity, and that such peer interactions fostered growth in intellectual self-concept (as well as retention in college, overall college satisfaction, and social self-concept) four years after college entry. Similarly, studies based on the National Study of Student Learning reveal that cognitive complexity measures are significantly associated with a variety of exposure and interaction variables, both after the first year of college (Pascarella et al. 1996) and in the second and third years of college (Whitt et al. 1998). In addition, the homogeneity of college peers (measured by participation in a sorority or fraternity) was negatively associated with this measure of students' cognitive complexity (Pascarella et al. 1996).

Utilizing a CIRP national sample of students different from the one identified for the legal cases, Hurtado (2001) found that students who studied frequently with someone from a different racial/ethnic background reported more growth on such learning self-assessments as problem-solving skills, general knowledge, critical thinking, foreign-language ability, writing skills, mathematical ability, and academic self-confidence. Similar kinds of effects have also been documented by Kuh (2003), using data from 285,000 students who answered the National Survey of Student Engagement. Kuh showed that students are more likely to be involved in active and collaborative learning when they are exposed to diversity.

Research on curricular initiatives that emphasize exposure to knowledge about race and ethnicity also supports our theoretical point of view about the potential impact of classroom diversity. Milem and Hakuta (2000) describe work carried out to evaluate a curricular project intended to infuse a diversity perspective into human development courses in college (MacPhee, Kreutzer, and Fritz 1994). This evaluation used both quantitative and qualitative methods to examine the impact of the curriculum transformation that occurred in these courses. The results show that the students had developed a number of critical thinking skills, that their levels of ethnocentrism had declined, and that they were able to make important distinctions between the causal meaning of poverty and the causal meaning of race/ethnicity as risk factors in the development of children. Additional support for the importance of curriculum can be found in an exhaustive review of evaluation studies of diversity programs, including multicultural education courses, carried out by Walter and Cookie Stephan (2001). Their review shows an overwhelmingly positive picture of the effects of curricular and cocurricular diversity programs. They examined thirty studies of long-term effects, all but two of them showing positive effects, as well as fifteen studies of short-term effects, none of which found negative effects.

Finally, two studies of short-term effects ask students themselves to assess the impact of diversity experience on their learning. One of these, a survey of law students attending the Harvard University and the University of Michigan law schools, shows that a very large majority of the students thought that discussing legal issues with diverse peers had significantly influenced their views of the law and their consideration of multiple perspectives (Orfield and Whitla 2001). For example, almost two-thirds of the students reported that "most of their classes were better because of diversity" and that they had personally benefited from this diversity. Because of the limited diversity in these schools, not all of the classes these students took were racially diverse. When law students were asked to compare their racially homogeneous classes with their diverse classes, 42 percent said that their diverse classes were superior in three ways: range of discussion, level of intellectual challenge, and seriousness with which alternative views were considered. Thus, an impressive proportion of these students attending two prestigious law schools believed that racial/ethnic diversity had enhanced their legal education.

A similar study was carried out on 639 medical students attending Harvard University and the University of California at San Francisco (Whitla et al. 2003). Nearly all of the students said that a diverse student body was a positive aspect of their educational experience. Eighty-four percent further thought that diversity had enhanced classroom discussion, and only 3 percent thought it had inhibited discussion. Eighty-six percent of the students also said that classroom diversity fostered serious discussion of alternative viewpoints.

All of these studies have been carried out with college students or with students in professional schools and thus were the most relevant to the affirmative action cases that concerned the use of race as one of many factors in college/law school admission. Additional relevant research, which has been carried out with students in K–12 schooling, was summarized in an amicus brief submitted to the Supreme Court by the National Education Association (Brief of Amici Curiae National Education Association at 8, *Grutter* [No. 02–241]). Reviewing these studies, the NEA concludes that "a racially diverse classroom remains the single best method for teaching our children to judge others as individuals, rather than according to stereotypes and prejudices. And, learning in a racially diverse setting furthers students' cognitive and intellectual development— thus providing an important educational benefit to all students, of every race" (10).

Is there no contrary evidence? Apart from critiquing our expert testimony (to which we return later), the opponents of affirmative action offered one study, published just a month before the Supreme Court hearing, which purportedly contradicted this wide body of research showing positive effects of experience with diversity. This study (Rothman et al. 2003) was based on a survey of 140 colleges and universities, sponsored by the National Association of Scholars, a major opponent of affirmative action and the source of amicus briefs submitted on behalf of the plaintiffs at the district, circuit, and Supreme Court levels. The study correlated an institution's percentage of African American students (ranging from 0 to 43 percent) with students' satisfaction with their education and students', faculty members', and administrators' perceptions of the quality of education at these schools. Perception of quality was represented by their judgments of the work habits and readiness of the students. The study shows that institutions with the largest proportion of African American students were viewed by students, faculty, and administrators as being of lower quality.

Three major problems with this study make it irrelevant to research on the educational value of diversity. First, there is a major flaw in their causal claims. Their central finding was this: "As the proportion of black students enrolled at the institution rose, student satisfaction with their university experience dropped, as did the assessments of the quality of their education, and the work efforts of their peers" (15). As Stephen Raudenbush (2003) points out, any reasonable reader would conclude that this study had found *increasing* diversity had harmed education. But, in fact, the authors simply compared 140 institutions *at a single point in time, and thus had no evidence about the effects of increasing diversity.*

Second, though the authors claim that the study addresses the issue of diversity, our arguments about the educational benefit of diversity include interaction between students of several groups, not merely African American students. Moreover, there is no measure in this study about actual interaction even between white and African American students. It depends entirely on students', faculty members', and administrators' perceptions of the quality of education in these schools.

Third, the study has no relevance to the central issue that was before the Supreme Court, using race as one of many factors in admission. The authors suggest that institutions serving large proportions of African American students suffer low quality *because of their affirmative action policies.* The study provides no basis for this assertion. Affirmative action exists only at predominantly white, selective, top-tier schools that use it to assure diversity. Schools that enroll more than about 8 to 10 percent African American students (generally the top percentage that selective institutions have been able to enroll, even with significant outreach efforts) have no relevance to the question that faced the Supreme Court because those schools do not use affirmative action in admission of students. "Yet precisely those schools (up to 43 percent African American enrollment) are driving the results of this study. Therefore, the Rothman study provides no basis for any conclusions about the potential benefits of adopting (or discarding) an affirmative action policy" (Raudenbush 2003).

What this study tells us is that faculty, students, and administrators were more critical of the quality of education in those schools that serve larger proportions of African American students. It tells us nothing about diversity or about the impact of affirmative action.

Democracy Outcomes

Our analyses show strong support for the role of diversity experience in helping students become active citizens and participants in a pluralistic democracy. (See Gurin et al. 2002 for the tabular presentation of the effects of different types of diversity experience on democracy outcomes.)

The same overall conclusions that we discerned for learning outcomes also describe the effects of diversity experience on democracy outcomes.

- The analyses show a pattern of consistent, positive relationships between democracy outcomes and students' experiences with diversity, and these effects apply across students in four ethnic/racial groups (African American, white, Latino(a)[8] and Asian American).
- The results are also consistently positive across multiple democracy outcome measures designed to capture students' citizenship engagement during college, racial/cultural engagement, motivation to take the perspective of others, and the belief that democracy and diversity can be compatible.
- The results are confirmed again in both the national and the local Michigan studies.
- Once again, the controls for students' democracy sentiments when they entered college assure us that the results can reasonably be talked about as having demonstrated effects of experience with diversity.

In the national study, students in all four groups (white, African American, Asian American, and Latino(a)) who had had the most experience with diversity were also the most engaged in various kinds of citizenship activities at the end of college. They were most committed to "influencing the political structure," "influencing social values," "helping others in difficulty," "being involved in programs to clean up the environment," and "participating in a community action program." Moreover, since we were able to control for the students' scores on the items that comprise citizenship engagement when they entered college, we know that experience with diverse peers produced an increase in their commitment to citizenship, as reflected in these kinds of activities. Diversity experience also had a clear impact on racial/cultural engagement as indicated by the students' assessments that they had become more "culturally aware and appreciative of cultural differences" as well as more "accepting of persons of different races and cultures." This effect was also consistent across all four racial/ethnic groups.

The results of the Michigan Student Study further support our claim that diversity experience influences democracy outcomes, in this instance three sentiments that we have argued are particularly important for citizenship in a heterogeneous democracy: perspective taking, the belief that democracy and difference can be compatible, and cultural engagement (learning about different groups in society). White, African American, and Asian American students who had the greatest amount of diversity experience—through classrooms, frequent and positive quality of interaction with diverse peers, greater exposure to multicultural events, and more involvement in intergroup dialogues—increased the most in their motivation to take the perspective of others. After controlling for their scores on these same items that comprise the perspective-taking measure at time of entrance, the students with the greatest amount of diversity experience at the University of Michigan most frequently said that they "try to look at everybody's side of a disagreement"; do not "find it difficult to see things from the other person's point of view"; "listen to other people's arguments"; and believe that there are "two sides to every question" and that they "try to look at them both."

The positive impact of diversity experience on what we call compatibility of difference and democracy is especially noteworthy because it specifically counters the charge made by some critics of affirmative action that using race as one of many factors in admission is divisive and threatens the commonality so needed in a democracy. This measure speaks directly to that charge. It includes questions that asked students to indicate how similar or different their own racial/ethnic group and other groups are in "important values in life—like values about work and family," as well as agreement/disagreement with the following four statements that assert the belief that difference brings divisiveness: "The University's focus on diversity puts too much emphasis on group differences," "The University's commitment to diversity fosters more intergroup division than understanding," "The University's emphasis on diversity means that I can't talk honestly about ethnic, racial, and gender issues," and "The emphasis on diversity makes it hard for me to be myself." For a high score on the compatibility measure, students have to perceive a lot of commonality between their own and other racial/ethnic groups and to *disagree* that an emphasis on diversity is divisive. African American, Asian American, and white students with the most experience with diversity expressed the greatest amount of commonality and least often found that diversity brought divisiveness—findings that are in complete opposition to claims frequently made against affirmative action and multicultural education. Since the assessments of commonality between one's own and other racial/ethnic groups were also asked at time of entrance and were used as controls in these analyses, it is reasonable to conclude that experience with diversity increased the students' sense that difference and democracy can be compatible.

Finally, Michigan students who had the most experience with diversity during college were the most culturally engaged, as indicated by their own assessments that they had learned the most "about other racial/ethnic groups during college."

These results repeatedly substantiate that actual experience with diversity fosters civic preparedness for participation in a diverse democracy where cultural competence, capacity to work well with people from various backgrounds, and consideration of multiple points of view are crucially needed.

Students' own statements also attest to learning that difference and commonality can be congenial and to gaining cultural competence skills through their interactions and genuine communication with diverse peers.

> The key thing that I have learned is that we all do have a lot of things in common. We can find that commonality, but we can only do that if we are willing to be aware of and respectful of each other's differences. I will carry that with me as I go into corporate life, and hopefully someday into politics as well.

As my generation enters the twenty-first century, we are faced with the challenge of communicating across racial, cultural, and social lines to understand one another in the midst of a multiracial, multi-class society. Naturally, we are all insecure with race relations because we don't want to risk our emotions or offend the opposite party. However, communication is now our only hope. We have to realize that to discuss race may be painful, scrutinizing, and even appalling, but we can be assured of ultimately reaching a better level of communication.

I have practically reinvented myself emotionally, socially, and intellectually in the last four years, primarily due to coming to terms with diversity and how I figure into it. I feel I can now work and be with anyone, and that certainly wasn't true when I came here four years ago. I have gotten leadership skills that I could not have dreamed about when I was in high school

An Educational Experiment in Diverse Democracy

Our expert testimony in the affirmative action cases included research that evaluated the effects of a particular curricular program at the University of Michigan (the Program on Intergroup Relations, IGR), which focuses on civic values, commitments, and capacities. Created by Michigan faculty in 1988 and offered regularly since then, primarily to incoming first-year students, it explicitly incorporates the conditions we have argued are important for diversity to have positive educational benefits: the presence of diverse peers, discontinuity from the precollege background, equality among peers, discussion under rules of civic discourse, and normalization and negotiation of conflict. It offers a sequence of course for undergraduates, beginning with an introductory course on intergroup relations and on conflict and community, and continuing through advanced courses for juniors and seniors.

The courses in IGR involve intergroup dialogues in which students from two identity groups (Latinos/as and Anglos, Arabs and Jews, African Americans and whites, women and men, etc.) are guided by trained undergraduate facilitators to talk across race and ethnicity (and across other differences as well) in the truly public way that is needed for a diverse democracy to work. They learn neither to ignore group differences, which many students tend to do in the service of individualism and color blindness, nor to privilege differences as ends in themselves. Benjamin Barber (1989) describes public talk as listening no less than speaking, involving affective as well as cognitive work, drawing people into the world of participation and action, and expressing ideas publicly rather than merely holding them privately.

The research included in the legal cases assessed the impact of the first course in this IGR sequence. It compared two groups of students, those who took the initial course, and a comparison group matched on gender, race/ethnicity, in-state and out-of-state precollege residency, and residence hall on campus. Both groups were part of the overall Michigan Student Study and thus had entrance data; they were both given questionnaires at the end of the first semester and again at the end of the senior year. Altogether 174 students, 87 participants and 87 nonparticipants, were in the study during their first year in college; 81 percent also were in the senior-year longitudinal follow-up study.

The first course reflected the emphasis in the entire program on the conditions that should have positive benefits on democracy outcomes. The participants (and the matched comparison group) came from *diverse backgrounds.* Slightly over a quarter were students of color; a third were men; and, 30 percent grew up in states other than Michigan. For nearly all of the students, this amount of diversity was quite *discrepant with their precollege backgrounds. Equality among peers* was assured in the intergroup dialogues that are an intrinsic part of the first course. These intergroup dialogues brought together an equal number of students (approximately eight) from two different identity groups that have had a history of disagreement over group-relevant experiences and policy issues (Zuñiga and Nagda 1993). For seven weeks, these groups engaged in weekly two-hour structured dialogues under clear *rules of civil discourse* such as listening respectfully to each other, making discussion a safe place for disagreements, disagreeing with ideas rather than with individuals, accepting expressions of emotion as legitimate and helpful, taking responsibility for one's own ideas and feelings by using "I" statements rather than attacking others, maintaining confidentiality for what is said within the group, and being honest rather than playing devil's advocate or other games. The participants were given the task of examining commonalities and differences between and within groups. *Conflict was normalized* through readings on the social functions of conflict, both positive and negative, and through simulations and exercises that taught communication and negotiation skills. (See Zuñiga, Nagda, and Sevig 2002 for more detailed description.)

The participants as seniors, *even after controlling for their responses to the entrance questionnaire*, showed, in comparison with nonparticipants, significantly greater

- Commitment to take the perspectives of others
- Sense of compatibility between difference and democracy as evidenced by sense of commonality in life values with other ethnic/racial groups and by the belief that difference is not necessarily divisive
- Positive evaluations of conflict as indicated, for example, in greater agreement/disagreement that "conflict and disagreements in classroom discussion enrich the learning process," and three other similar statements (some phrased negatively such as "I learned that conflict rarely has constructive consequences")
- Mutuality in learning about own and other groups as reflected in learning about the history and experiences of

other groups as well as about their own group, and partici-
pating in activities of other groups as well as activities of their
own groups
* Interest in politics
* Racial/cultural engagement
* Participation in campus political groups

The two groups did not differ, however, in how much they had
participated in student government or in community service activities. (See Gurin, Nagda, and Lopez 2004 for a detailed presentation of the effects of the IGR on preparation for citizenship over
four years of college.)

Research of Other Scholars on Democracy Outcomes

Supportive evidence from other scholars is only now beginning to
accumulate. It is not only that scholarship probing how diversity
relates to civic education has been extremely limited, but also that
until recently social science has given remarkably little attention to
the processes by which young people become educated as democratic citizens, with or without considering the issue of diversity. In
an introduction to a collection of essays in the *Journal of Social
Issues* addressing this neglect, Flanagan and Sherrod (1998) concluded that "research on the developmental correlates of civic competence or the processes by which children become members of
political communities has, to say the least, not been a prominent
theme in the social sciences" (447).

Recent work on youth political development, which has mostly
been carried out with high school youth, shows that youth who
participate in volunteer work, organized groups, community service, and political activities are more likely to be active citizens as
adults (Flanagan and Sherrod 1998; Youniss and Yates 1997; Yates
and Youniss 1999). The lasting impact of participation as a youth

results from learning the organizational practices that are required in adult citizen activities and from establishing a civic identity during an opportune moment in the formation of identity (Youniss, McClellan, and Yates 1997). Civic development is fostered by family values and practices that emphasize social responsibility (Flanagan and Sherrod 1998), by families with higher education and income (Flanagan and Tucker 1999), and by school climates that encourage expression of opinions and identification with the school (Flanagan and Sherrod 1998).

Of course, there is a large body of literature on the impact of college on aspects of student development that relate to civic identity. A major review of college impact studies carried out by Pascarella and Terenzini (1991) showed that higher education fosters altruistic, humanitarian, and civic values, as well as greater tolerance and principled reasoning in judging moral issues (for a different view suggesting that adults with college education and even postcollege education are not more tolerant than less educated Americans, see Jackman and Muha 1984). In the college studies, the weight of the evidence suggests that a statistically significant, if modest, part of the broad-based changes in attitudes, values, and moral reasoning occurring during college can be attributed to the college experience and is not simply a reflection of trends in the larger society (Terenzini et al. 1994). Reviewing national sample studies and a multicity study of whites, African Americans, Latinos(as), and Asian Americans, Bobo and colleagues (2000) substantiate that education fosters more tolerant racial outlooks.

It is important to note that neither the recent research on high school youth nor the longer-standing research on college youth has examined the influence of experience with diversity as a socializing influence for civic preparedness. Studies specifically on the impact of diversity on preparation for citizenship, or what we are calling democracy outcomes, are just beginning to appear in the social science literature. Among these, Hurtado (2001) found that interaction across race/ethnicity, as evident in studying with someone from a different racial/ethnic background, positively influenced measures of civic engagement. Another national study extended these findings and showed that students with a high proportion of diverse close friends in college reported growth in leadership and cultural knowledge after four years of college (Antonio 2001). Chang and colleagues (2002) further document other studies that have found a link between curricular initiatives as well as interaction with diverse peers and what broadly might be called cultural competence. One of these studies (Chang, Astin, and Kim 2004) found that students who had interacted the most across racial groups also reported that they had grown the most in their ability to get along with people from different races/cultures while being more likely to vote, volunteer, and participate in community action. Further, the results show that, after adjusting for how students saw themselves upon entry into college, the students with the most cross-racial interaction ended college with an increased sense of themselves as leaders and as empathetic with others. These effects of cross-racial interaction persisted, moreover, when Chang and colleagues took account of various personal characteristics of the students at time of entrance and of the same kind of institutional characteristics that our analyses adjusted for as well.

Making deeper friendships and becoming more comfortable in cross-racial relationships because of an initial interaction that lasts over time is especially well demonstrated in an experimental study conducted by Duncan and colleagues (2003).

This study took advantage of the fact that a portion of incoming first-year students at a large midwestern university are randomly assigned roommates. (The remaining students either asked to room with a friend from home or selected singles.) The random assignment provided a natural experiment in which students were either randomly given a roommate of their own or a different racial/ethnic background. Students lived together throughout the first year of college. Responses to questionnaires administered to these students during the first year of college and two and four years later showed that white students[9] who were randomly assigned room-mates of color were more comfortable than the other white students were with people of other races in their later years of college; they also had more personal contact across race and ethnicity. White students who were randomly assigned African American roommates, in contrast to those who were randomly assigned white roommates, more frequently considered their roommate to be a best friend during the first year of college. Causality is clear in this study. These students were not selecting roommates but simply lived with a person randomly given to them. A year-long living experience with a roommate from a different racial/ethnic background demonstrably affected these students' comfort and abilities to get along across racial lines.

The students at Harvard and University of Michigan law schools who were studied by Orfield and Whitla (2001) related in their subjective evaluations of the impact of diversity that it had affected their "ability to work more effectively and/or get along better with members of other races." Sixty-eight percent of the Harvard law students and 48 percent of the Michigan law students saw a clear, positive impact of this sort. Seventy-six percent of the students in the Whitla et al. (2003) medical school survey reported that experience with diversity helped them work more effectively with those of diverse racial backgrounds.

In the racially/ethnically diverse society that the United States already is, this effect of diversity experience during college augurs well for achieving the understanding, comfort, and integration of both difference and similarities that will be needed to make a diverse democracy work. Studies of racial stereotypes and the role of interracial contact in reducing stereotypes are particularly important in realizing this goal, as stereotypes stand in the way of understanding and stem from and reinforce exaggerated conceptions of difference. The work that we presented to the Supreme Court did not include measures of stereotypes, but a rich research literature on the subject can be found within social psychology.

The amicus brief submitted to the Supreme Court by the American Psychological Association (Brief of Amici Curiae American Psychological Association at 5–6, *Grutter* [No. 02–241]) summarizes the important findings from this literature. The APA draws four basic conclusions.

- First, racial prejudice and stereotypes are widespread in the United States, although they are now less blatant and more unconscious than the old fashioned racism was (Dovidio and Gaertner 2000; Spencer et al. 1998; Blascovich et al. 1997; Devine 1989; Dovidio et al. 1997). That implicit prejudice and stereotypes operate in the unconscious mind does not mean that they do not affect behavior or that they cannot be altered.
- Second, automatic prejudice plays an important role in producing discriminatory behavior and judgments (Fazio and Olson 2003; McConnell and Liebold 2001; von Hippel, Sekaquaptewa, and Vargas 1997; Sekaquaptewa et al. 2003; Dovidio et al. 2002).
- Third, there is clear evidence that implicit prejudice and stereotypes become exaggerated for token minorities in groups. That is the reason that the University of Michigan has stressed the importance of having a "critical mass" of students of color, a topic that we return to below in addressing criticisms of our work and the university's case.
- Fourth, unconscious prejudice and stereotypes *can* be altered. There is considerable research undertaken recently showing that unconscious stereotyping can be offset or reduced through positive exposure to members of other racial groups (Blair 2002). It is "face to face interaction that . . . is importantly related to reduced prejudice" (Pettigrew and Tropp 2000, 109).

The APA's analysis of the prevalence, behavioral implications, and alterations of unconscious prejudice and stereotypes is completely consistent with the emphasis that we, and other scholars, have placed on *actual experience* with diverse others. If our students are to learn how to understand each other and work together across race and ethnicity, as preparation for citizen and leadership roles in a diverse democracy, they must have curricular and cocurricular opportunities and encouragement for that to happen. It is not simply the number of years of schooling that is correlated with reduced stereotyping, but rather the kind of schooling that students have been afforded.

Finally, the extensive study of students at selective institutions conducted by Bowen and Bok (1998) supports the evidence we have presented on the long-term impact of college diversity experience on democracy outcomes. Bowen and Bok show, for example, that nearly half of the white students and over half of the African American students in the 1976 cohort who had attended diverse, selective institutions reported in the later follow-up study that their undergraduate experience had been of considerable value in "developing their ability to work with, and get along with, people of different races and cultures." The percentages who claimed this effect were even greater among the 1989 cohort of students attending selective, diverse institutions: 63 percent of the white graduates and 70 percent of the African American graduates. The Bowen and Bok study further shows that the long-term benefits of a diverse student body were evident not only in terms of the graduates' self-assessed capacity to work with diverse others and of academic and economic outcomes for individuals but also in terms of leadership in diverse communities and in contributions to social service organizations. African American men in particular who had attended selective colleges were likely as adults to be involved in civic activities in their communities—more so than white men who had attended the same colleges, and more so than African American men who had gone to less selective institutions. While these findings are not direct evidence that experience with diversity produces civic engagement after college, they do show a positive impact of attending institutions that were employing affirmative action policies and procedures to achieve diverse student bodies.

How Diversity Experience Affects Students

We have seen in the analyses we carried out of the national and local Michigan data and in the research of other scholars, much of it summarized in social science amicus briefs to the Supreme Court, that experience with diverse peers has many positive benefits for students. In the period following the Supreme Court decision, research will increasingly turn to understanding the *processes* by which these effects occur. There are already a few studies on processes, all of which emphasize the crucial importance of friendships, personal relationships, and sharing of stories and experiences across race/ethnicity.

Two studies carried out on the Program on Intergroup Relations examined what aspects of the courses—content (as presented through lectures and readings), and active learning techniques (as presented through experiential exercises and daily writing in a reflection journal)—accounted for the effects on learning and democracy outcomes. (See Lopez, Gurin, and Nagda 1998; Nagda, Gurin, and Lopez 2003.) In general, both content and active learning techniques were influential, but active learning techniques were especially important in the recommendations students made about what should be done to deal with intergroup conflicts that sometimes take place on college campuses (Lopez et al. 1998). Students who were the most involved in classroom exercises and journal reflections were the most likely to endorse institutional approaches for solving intergroup conflicts. Actual practice in analyzing simulated campus conflicts and exploring actions through role playing and other active learning exercises were crucial for going beyond the simplest, most individual solutions. Lectures and readings *alone* cannot provide this kind of learning. Kolb (1984), an important theorist of active learning, says that the cyclical nature of learning in which reflection, dialogue, and action reinforce each other can be generated by having students bring their lived experiences into the classroom and subjecting them to reflection and experimentation, as well as by taking what they learn in class to the outside world for confirmation, disconfirmation, and refinement of theory.

Students attest to the importance of learning from each other through open discussion.

> Listening and doing things together—those are the keys.

> You have to be in a multi-cultural/racial class of students who are willing to be open-minded and honest with each other. They have to listen to each other and work, discuss, and be together. Professors have to be ready to make that happen.

> By laying race out on the table and talking straight with others who are different from you, you become aware of how little you understood before, and sensitivity is formed. This can be done in classes, like this class. It can be done in the residence halls. But it has to be done.

A qualitative study, conducted by Anna Yeakley (1998) with students who took the IGR courses at the University of Michigan, also provides insight into the processes by which intergroup dialogue affects students. She focused on both positive and negative impact, and found two important results. First, the majority of the changes that the students said they had undergone in intergroup dialogues were positive. Second and more importantly, it was the extent to which students established intimate contact with diverse peers that distinguished positive from negative outcomes. Intimate contact was indicated by depth of personal sharing of their life stories, of reactions to each other, and of emotions engendered in the classroom discussions. The importance of intimacy has been recognized ever since Allport wrote on contact and prejudice (1954), although contact theorists have not always specified it in measurable behavioral terms. Yeakley stresses that intimate contact goes beyond merely knowing others as individuals and involves in-depth personal sharing and self-disclosure of group-related experiences. Two students talk about such personal sharing, and especially about the importance of sharing emotions:

> To have people tell you how they feel about something, it just makes you empathize, like you know the person and not just a name.

> With personal experience, you can be as emotional as you want to be, because it's your emotions, and we understand that. And, you are a real person who had a real experience.

Yeakley emphasizes that self-disclosure in personal sharing does not happen unless interaction in a class is frequent, direct, involves listening as well as talking, and is respectful and inquiring rather than critical and judgmental.

The importance of personal sharing is also seen in a study of the student facilitators of the intergroup dialogues who are an intrinsic part of the IGR courses. Before the facilitators actually lead an intergroup dialogue, they enroll in a semester-long training course that meets weekly for three hours. Then, during the semester that they facilitate a dialogue, they also enroll in another course that provides close supervision, group discussion of effective and ineffective dialogue processes, and advanced readings on intergroup relations. Carolyn Vasquez-Scalera (1999) studied the experience of facilitation across four years of the IGR, fall 1992 through winter 1996. The student facilitators consistently stressed that the effect of the facilitation experience resulted from being part of a learning community in which personal, emotional, and experiential learning were nurtured, along with traditional kinds of academic learning.

The importance of personal sharing is supported by recent research on intimate relationships in settings other than classrooms—in families, friendships in adult life, work settings (Aron et al. 1991, 1992, 1997; McAdams 1988; Reis and Shaver 1988). This research defines intimacy as sharing innermost feelings, being validated and understood by others, and validating and understanding others. The role of personal sharing is also supported by research on intergroup attitudes that is reviewed by Pettigrew (1998). He highlights the central importance of friendships involving personal sharing with people of a different race, religion, class, or culture in accounting for positive intergroup attitudes. Such friendships, he argues, allow the development of empathy between people with different life experiences.

Is it possible, or even appropriate, for college classrooms to provide a medium for this kind of personal sharing and self-disclosure? Some faculty will not see this as their responsibility. Some would not know how to incorporate discussion that involves sharing of life experiences and emotions, even if they thought it was educationally beneficial. Some faculty disapprove of personal sharing and emotions in academic classrooms. Still, other faculty are comfortable with providing opportunities for these more personal and emotional aspects of learning, and when they do, a growing body of research confirms that sharing, reflection, and dialoguing (especially when it is integrated with content through lectures, readings, and didactic learning) can be a powerful educational tool. Moreover, as we have repeatedly stressed, students also learn from each other in the informal campus world, and it is there that structured opportunities for intergroup dialogue involving personal sharing, self-disclosure, and emotions can be extremely influential.

Answering Our Critics

We submitted our expert testimony containing our theoretical rationale and the empirical evidence in December 1998. Although the Center for Individual Rights offered no rebuttal witness and conceded the educational value of diversity in the two cases at the district court, it did submit critiques of our work that were conducted by the National Association of Scholars (NAS), a national organization of politically conservative academics. The critiques were appended to amicus briefs that the NAS provided for the CIR appeal to the Sixth Circuit Court of Appeals, and to the Supreme Court. Those critiques (Wood and Sherman 2001, 2003; Lerner and Nagai 2001, 2003; and some others by opponents of affirmative action) have raised important and interesting issues about the educational value of diversity to which we now turn. We responded to these critiques on Michigan's website (Gurin 2001, 2003; Gurin, Gurin, and Matlock 2003), and we address them below by asking and answering a series of questions.[10]

Why focus on the experiences students have with diversity? Isn't the controversy about racial and ethnic composition in the study body?

The key conclusion emerging from our work and the work of other social scientists is that it is *actual experience* with diverse peers that is important for educational outcomes. The University of Michigan has a deliberate policy, not only of building a diverse student body, but also of promoting diversity experiences for students that in turn are related to educational outcomes. This is not a policy of simply recruiting a diverse student body and then neglecting the intellectual environment in which students interact. Like all resources, structural diversity must be used intelligently to fulfill its potential.

Some critics in amicus briefs to the court argued that the presence of ethnically and racially diverse students must *by itself* be sufficient for achieving desired outcomes if the university policies were to be justified. But if that were true, then having good buildings, high faculty salaries, and good libraries would all be sufficient to ensure a good education. No one with the responsibility to run a university would make such an argument, precisely because the nature of educational activities and the extent to which students avail themselves of these resources are crucial to achieving an excellent education.

Justice Powell's decisive statement, providing the diversity rationale for the use of race in the *Bakke* case (312), made clear that actual interaction with diverse peers, and not their mere presence on the campus, is precisely how diversity affects students. He included in his opinion a quotation from William Bowen, then president of Princeton University, to that effect.

> The president of Princeton University has described some of the benefits derived from a diverse student body: A great deal of learning occurs informally. It occurs through interactions among students of both sexes; of different races, religions, and backgrounds; who come from cities and rural areas, from various states and countries; who have a wide variety of interests, talents, and perspectives; and who are able, directly or indirectly, to learn from their differences and to stimulate one another to reexamine even their most deeply held assumptions about themselves and their world. As a wise graduate of ours observed in commenting on this aspect of the educational process, "People do not learn very much when they are surrounded only by the likes of themselves." (Bowen 1977, 9)

Our emphasis on diversity experiences follows the logic of Justice Powell as to how a diverse student body improves understanding and personal growth. The rich body of research on interracial contact supports the importance of actual interaction, especially when it occurs between members of equal status groups that have common goals, and when the interaction is based on cooperation rather than competition and is endorsed and legitimated by authorities. In these conditions, members of different groups can get to know each other as individuals (Allport 1954; Amir 1976; Cook 1984; Pettigrew 1998; Stephan and Stephan 2001). Not surprisingly, research on higher education also shows that institutions must create opportunities for students to have these kinds of interactions. The University of Michigan is one of those institutions that has created opportunities in classes and in the informal student environment for interaction of diverse students to affect student learning and preparation for participation in a democratic society.

If racial and ethnic diversity isn't sufficient by itself, is it important to defend policies to assure that it exists in a university? Do universities have to have students from diverse backgrounds to produce educational benefits for students?

Some of the critics of the university's policies argue, in effect, that a student can have experience with diversity without diverse others (Wood and Sherman 2001, 2003). The critics seem to believe that any effects we demonstrated could result simply from readings, lectures, and teaching *about* race and ethnicity. We have shown, especially in the national study, that the larger effects come from interaction with diverse peers in the informal educational world of the campus. Moreover, we have shown in the Michigan studies, where we know much more about what diversity in the classroom means, that courses that cover content knowledge about racial and ethnic groups also generally attract diverse students. We know that the courses that met the requirement in the College of Letters, Sciences, and Arts to take at least one course that covers race and ethnicity were composed of diverse students. The Michigan measure of classroom diversity is actually a combination, therefore, of course content about race and interaction with diverse peers in the classroom.

We also know as teachers of courses that address race and ethnicity that learning from peers and especially from diverse peers is vitally important in our undergraduate classroom. In a first-year seminar on groups and community that Patricia Gurin has taught for several years, a particularly poignant class event revealed the power of real interaction with diverse peers.

The class focused on the cultural value of individualism and the role of groups within an individualistic culture. In general, students find the idea of groups a bit uncomfortable. They long to be just individuals, which, of course, they are even as they are also members of race, class, gender, age, geographic, religious, and other groups. In this class session, a white woman student who had grown up in a homogeneously white town in Michigan expressed, with considerable emotion, that she was tired of being categorized as white.

> I'm just an individual. No one knows if I hold similar beliefs to those of other white students just by looking at me. I hate being seen just as white.

She ended in tears. An African American male student who had grown up in a virtually all-white city in Connecticut replied as he walked toward her across the classroom.

> I just want to be an individual also. But every day as I walk across this campus—just as I am walking across this room right now—I am categorized. No one knows what my thoughts are, or if my thoughts align with other African American students. They just see me as a black male. And at night, they often change their pace to stay away from me. The point is—groups do matter. They matter in my life and (as he approached the other student whose hand he then took), they matter in your life.

There was silence in the room. The students learned about the meaning of groups and the meaning of individuals in a way that they won't soon forget.

This could not have been taught from a lecture. Real interaction with diverse others in a classroom made this learning powerful and indelible.

This conclusion is supported by research of other scholars, summarized in the amicus brief of the National Education Association

(Brief of Amici Curiae National Education Association at 8, *Grutter* [No. 02–241]), as well as by our research and teaching experience.

How much is enough? Even if affirmative action is needed for the current amount of diversity at the University, is that amount of diversity *enough?* Is the current probability of interacting with diverse peers achievable in a race-blind admission policy?

It is impossible for social science to provide a precise answer *to the question of what level of diversity is necessary to achieve positive benefits.* It is possible, however, to show how changing the admissions policy to be race-blind would have markedly affected the experience of both white and underrepresented minority students. Figure 1 shows that under a race-blind admissions policy, the opportunity for a white student to interact with at least three underrepresented students is dramatically *decreased,* and essentially disappears in *small* educational settings, such as a first-year seminar, student government, intramural sports teams, and student activity groups. Figure 2 shows that the probability of an underrepresented minority student being the *only one* in particular educational settings is dramatically *increased* under race-blind admissions. We have emphasized these particular probabilities because research in social psychology demonstrates over many studies that solos (the only one) and tokens (a tiny minority) are highly visible, evaluated in extreme ways, and perceived in stereotyped ways. This research has also shown that majority group members are prone to stereotypic evaluations in situations where they greatly outnumber the number of minority individuals. Interacting with at least three minority individuals allows majority group members to see that not all minority individuals are alike.

In addition to changing student experiences, a few conclusions are clear from understanding how the campus would have changed under a race-blind policy. First, the University of Michigan has achieved significant educational benefits from the levels of under-represented minority students on campus that have resulted from using race as one of many factors in admissions (ranging between 12 percent and 16 percent of the undergraduate student body in recent years, and 25 percent if Asian American students are included). Second, Michigan's level of diversity under its race-conscious admission policies has not achieved all of the potential benefits available to the university. Increasing the level of diversity would provide additional opportunities for interactions in classrooms and informal settings, which are critical to the success of the mission of higher education. Third, Michigan's admission policies that were challenged in court produced percentages of underrepresented minorities that are far from achieving the composition that social psychologists have found to be the ideal—balanced ratios of group members—nor was anyone from the university advocating balanced ratios (Mullen and Hu 1989). Fourth, it is clear that the educational benefits we have demonstrated were much at risk in the legal challenge to which the University of Michigan responded.

What about other kinds of diversity? Why is racial/ethnic diversity so important?

Other kinds of diversity *are* important. The Law School and the Undergraduate Admission Offices recruit and admit students from many different kinds of backgrounds: international, rural, working-class, precollege residency in Michigan from counties other than the five southeastern counties that comprise most of the university's undergraduate students, states other than Michigan, and states other than the other five in which most of Michigan's out-of-state students grew up. The university's effort to enroll students from all of these various backgrounds diversifies what would otherwise be a student body predominantly from the United States, urban settings, the state of Michigan (and the states of New York, Illinois, California, New Jersey, and Ohio), and middle-class and

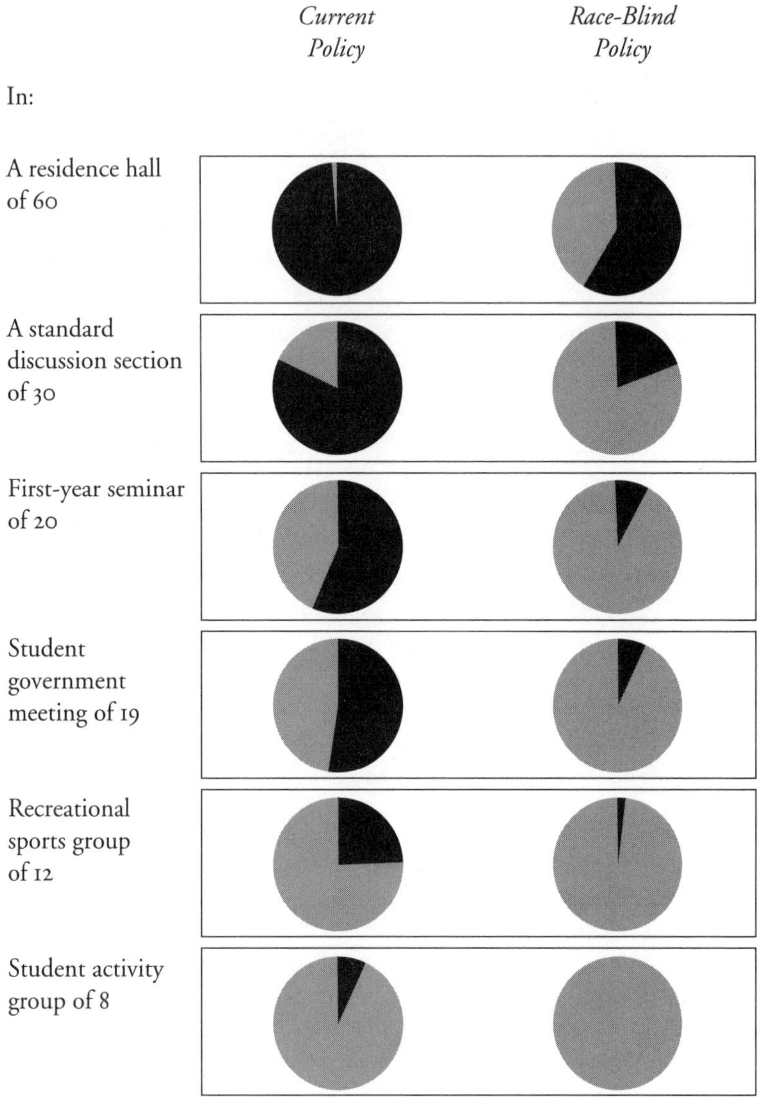

| | *Current Policy* | *Race-Blind Policy* |

In:

A residence hall of 60

A standard discussion section of 30

First-year seminar of 20

Student government meeting of 19

Recreational sports group of 12

Student activity group of 8

FIGURE 1. A day in the life of a white undergraduate

Area in black shows the probability of interacting with
at least 3 underrepresented minority students

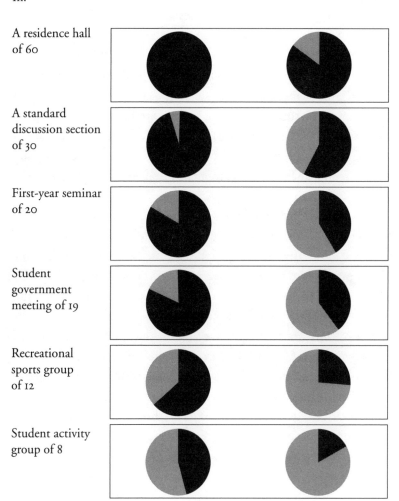

	Current Policy	Race-Blind Policy

In:

A residence hall of 60

A standard discussion section of 30

First-year seminar of 20

Student government meeting of 19

Recreational sports group of 12

Student activity group of 8

FIGURE 2. A day in the life of an underrepresented
minority student

Area in black shows the probability of not being a solo:
The only underrepresented minority student

upper-middle-class economic situations. Admissions staff also recruit students with a wide range of talents and interests within all of these demographic categories.

Race, however, is *the* major social divide in the United States. Thomas Sugrue (1999) documents racial segregation and isolation in contemporary United States. He points out that even as the United States becomes increasingly diverse, the vast majority of African Americans and Latinos(as) are concentrated in certain regions, within those regions often in certain states, and within those states in particular urban areas. Looking just at the state of Michigan, where two-thirds of the university's undergraduates grow up, Sugrue further documents widespread within-state segregation.

This concentration of minority groups in particular areas in Michigan means that the vast majority of Michigan's eighty-three counties have tiny minority populations. Moreover, within the eleven metropolitan areas where minority groups reside in Michigan, residential segregation virtually assures that most whites and African Americans interact minimally in their daily lives.

The history of race, ethnicity, and education in the United States, described in depth by Lewis (in this volume), coupled with the profound racial isolation that continues to be the experience of most Americans and certainly of the students who come to the University of Michigan, makes racial/ethnic diversity unlike any other dimension of diversity in our nation.

Don't race-conscious policies and a focus on diversity have harmful effects as well? Doesn't a focus on race/ethnicity stigmatize students of color?

Some critics of affirmative action in higher education argue that it undermines the performance of minority students, and causes them to be stigmatized, become demoralized, and drop out of college.

In their classic book, *The Shape of the River*, Bowen and Bok

(1998) demonstrate just the opposite. African American students were not demoralized, nor did they drop out of college at highly selective colleges where affirmative action had been in place more often than at less selective colleges. Bowen and Bok show that African American students *within every SAT interval* graduated at higher rates from elite schools than African American students attending nonselective schools. They also show that African Americans at highly selective institutions were just as likely as whites at these schools to attend the most competitive professional schools and to become doctors, lawyers, and business executives. Moreover, these kinds of successes characterized African American students who graduated from highly selective institutions more than their African American peers, with comparable SAT scores, who graduated from less selective four-year institutions. All of these findings in *Shape of the River* contradict the idea that African American students who attended the most selective institutions were harmed by the affirmative action policies that operated in the admission of some of them. African American students were not better off educationally in less selective institutions where the average SAT scores matched their own.

What do students of color themselves think of affirmative action? A number of studies show that they are aware that this policy allows white students to doubt that they, the minority, are as capable as majority students. Yet, while they acknowledge that others may doubt their abilities, these studies also show that students of color believe that other people doubt their abilities *regardless* of affirmative action. In other words, they understand that it is their minority status itself—not affirmative action policies—that sometimes causes them to be stigmatized (Downing et al. 2002).

In the Michigan Student Study, African American students in particular were aware that they were stigmatized by others, both other students and faculty members. For example, 59 percent of the African American seniors (in contrast to 26 percent of the Latino/a, 14 percent of the Asian American, and 15 percent of the white seniors) agreed that "I have encountered faculty and students who feel that I don't have a right to be here." In response to another question, only 27 percent of the African American seniors (in contrast to 76 percent of the Latino/a, 70 percent of the Asian American, and 84 percent of the white seniors) felt that the Michigan climate reflected "quite a bit" or "a great deal" of "respect by white faculty for students of color." However, this latter question was also asked on the entrance survey. The responses indicate that a large majority of African American students did not *expect* to encounter much respect from white faculty, even before they had any experience in the university. When asked about what they expected to find at Michigan, only 39 percent of the African American students (in contrast to 70 percent of the Latino/a, 73 percent of the Asian American, and 86 percent of the white entering students) said that they expected "quite a bit" or "a great deal" of "respect by white faculty for students of color." Although there is a 12 percent increase in feelings of devaluation among African American students over the four years of college, the feelings they expressed as seniors were largely a function of what they thought would happen at Michigan when they came as entering freshmen. For most African American students, feelings of devaluation do not suddenly appear in college because of affirmative action. (There is also, of course, no evidence that the 12 percent increase among African Americans in feelings of faculty disrespect can be attributed to affirmative action, or any other particular cause.)

Psychologist Faye Crosby (2004), in a thorough analysis of reactions to affirmative action, draws conclusions from her work and the research of other scholars on stigmatization, conducted both in the laboratory and in actual employment and higher education settings.

- There is evidence that people stigmatize recipients of affirmative action *unless* it is made very clear that these recipients are highly competent.

- Stigmatization does negatively affect performance and self-confidence, although stigmatization and stereotyping of women and persons of color exist even when there is no reference to affirmative action. Stigmatization and stereotyping are part of racism in the United States.
- Self-doubts among recipients of affirmative action exist but are not pronounced or widespread. Creation of self-doubts from affirmative action is generally not the devastating problem that some famous writers—Richard Rodriguez (1981), Shelby Steele (1990), and Stephen Carter (1991) and Supreme Court Justice Clarence Thomas in his dissenting opinion in *Grutter v. Bollinger* say that it has been in their lives.
- Studies of minority college/university students, of minority workers in employment settings, and of minority adults in national sample surveys show in general that they approve of affirmative action (though definitely not of racial/ethnic quotas), believe they have benefited from it, and do not feel stigmatized from the presence of gender-sensitive or race-sensitive policies.

There is a clear message in Crosby's thorough analysis of the pluses and minuses of race-sensitive policies. Perhaps the most critical for higher education is the significance of being absolutely clear that students admitted under such policies are completely qualified to perform, to graduate from undergraduate schools, to obtain higher education, to achieve in later life, and to contribute to society. That is certainly the case at the University of Michigan.

Don't affirmative action and a focus on diversity produce racial/ethnic hostility on college campuses? Aren't these race-conscious policies inevitably divisive?

We have argued that racial/ethnic diversity in an institution increases the likelihood that students will have experience with diversity in classrooms and in intergroup interactions that are positive, cooperative, and personal. One frequent criticism of affirmative action is that it does not foster these positive interactions, but on the contrary creates a racial campus climate of intergroup hostility, tension, and conflict.

This criticism was a major point made by Robert Lerner and Althea Nagai in an amicus brief filed by the National Association of Scholars (NAS). Lerner and Nagai argue that affirmative action and a campus focus on multiculturalism and diversity have negative effects on intergroup relationships because they heighten the salience of the boundaries between groups. They also claim that affirmative action subverts the most important precondition for having a positive impact from intergroup interaction—that the group participants be equal in status—because they contend that differences in average SAT scores between African Americans and white students make equality in relationships impossible. They conclude that "if one applies the notion of equal status contact properly, achieving social diversity by means of racial and ethnic preferences will not only fail to foster intergroup cooperation but will enhance mutual suspicion and hostility between racial and ethnic groups" (47).

Despite years of controversy about affirmative action and its impact, and the abundance of anecdotal evidence brought to this debate, there is little systematic, quantitative evidence on the nature of intergroup relationships on college campuses in the United States. A number of questions in the surveys of the Michigan Student Study (MSS) directly address the issue of campus climate and personal intergroup relationships. The students' responses to these questions do not support the critics' views of the negative state of intergroup relationships on such campuses, at least not on the Michigan campus.

In general, the great majority of white students as well as students of color feel that their relationships with other racial/ethnic groups on campus have been predominantly positive. About 90 percent of Asian American, Latino/a, and white students, and about 80 percent of African American students agreed as seniors that "My relationships with students from different racial/ethnic groups at the University have been positive." Most compelling are the students' responses to a question that asked them about their relationships with the racial/ethnic group they interacted with the most on the Michigan campus. The question presented a list of positive and negative intergroup interactions (e.g., "studied together," "shared our personal feelings and problems," "had guarded, cautious interactions," "had tense, somewhat hostile interactions") and asked students to what extent these types of interactions characterized their relationships with students in that group.

The quality of intergroup interactions that emerged from the responses to this question was strikingly positive, particularly between white, Asian American, and Latino/a students. White students view their relationships with Asian American and Latino/a students, and Asian Americans and Latinos/as view their relationships with whites, as involving considerable cooperation and personal sharing, as well as very little hostility and tension. Relationships that white students had with African American students were somewhat less personal than their relationships with other students of color, but very few white students felt that their interactions with African American students were negative. African American students reported that their relationships with white students were somewhat ambivalent, with approximately the same percentage of African American students characterizing their relationships with white students as negative and as positive.

The greater distance in the relationships between African American and white students is not surprising, reflecting as it does the legacy of our long troubled national history of black-white relationships. More surprising is that so few white students, less than 5 percent, experienced these relationships as cautious, tense, or hostile. These findings question the claim of critics of diversity that affirmative action has poisoned the racial climate on campuses, that in particular it has evoked negative, hostile reactions of white students because of their feelings of resentment at so-called reverse discrimination, and their supposed negative campus experiences with "unqualified" students admitted because of racial preference. None of these claims are supported by systematic data from students' experiences in intergroup relations on campus.

The students' responses to other questions from the MSS provide further evidence that discredits the claim that affirmative action has produced a white student "backlash." While the majority of white students, as well as students of color, agree in principle that racial/ethnic inequalities exist in higher education and that universities have a responsibility to address these inequities, it is true that there are great racial/ethnic group differences in responding to specific questions about addressing inequality in higher education. Many fewer white students than students of color support specific affirmative action policies that universities like the University of Michigan have undertaken to address these inequalities. However, these great group differences are apparent in the way that students think about such policies when they entered the University of Michigan and thus before they encountered the campus diversity produced by affirmative action. For the white students at Michigan, 90 percent of whom come from segregated neighborhoods and high schools, this means that their lack of support for affirmative action derives primarily from their precollege social environments and the ways in which affirmative action issues have been framed in the public debate, and not from negative experiences with diversity during their college years. For this reason, it is important to review longitudinal data on students, to understand how students change their initial perspectives, often adopting a more complex understanding of racial issues in society. There is little support in the MSS findings for the criticism that affirmative action policies to achieve diversity cause a "backlash," particularly among white students, because of their interactions with what the opponents of affirmative action consider unqualified minority students.

The MSS results in fact show the opposite, that the changes that do occur after four years at Michigan are in the direction of *greater support* for affirmative action student admission policies. This is true for all groups of students. Their attitude changes on admission criteria are particularly relevant since they were the focus of the legal challenge to affirmative action in higher education. All in all, the picture of intergroup relationships on the Michigan campus that emerges from the MSS, and the role of affirmative action in affecting these relationships, do not support the negative picture presented by the critics of affirmative action.

The charge of extensive racial hostility, tension, and conflict on campuses where affirmative action is used in admissions is not borne out in our systematic survey of Michigan. A critical question is why the negative view prevails. It persists, we believe, because there has been so little systematic research and because journalists, critics of affirmative action, and ordinary citizens have reverted to using anecdotes, frequently repeating anecdotes that have made their way from one newspaper, television, or magazine article to another.

Responses to another MSS question further illuminate the question of why the negative view prevails so widely and over time. A question on "racial climate" presented students with a list of phrases and asked them the extent to which each of them was descriptive of the University of Michigan campus. Slightly over one-quarter of the white students responded that there was "quite a bit" or "a great deal" of "interracial tension on campus." Although this does not indicate widespread perception of racial tension, it is considerably more than the 4 percent of white students who actually reported "tense, somewhat hostile interactions" in their own relationships with students of color. Their responses reveal that the fairly common belief that there is widespread racial tension on our college campuses is overgeneralization from anecdotal and focus group research, rather than systematic survey research, and from highly publicized ugly racial incidents that have occurred on some campuses, rather than reflections of the students' personal day-to-day experiences with interracial relationships.

Even if racial tension on university campuses were greater than the MSS data suggest, we find it somewhat puzzling that critics of affirmative action have focused so much on this issue. One should not be surprised that *perception of some racial tension* exists at Michigan or that such perceptions might be expressed by more students on campuses where commitment to racial/ethnic diversity is strong. Nearly all of Michigan's white students and half of the African American students came to Michigan (at the time of the MSS) with practically no experience with diverse peers. They had little to anchor their perceptions. Nor is it surprising that *perception of racial tension* increases somewhat over the four years in college on campuses, including the University of Michigan, where the issue of race is highly salient. If perceptions of racial tension had resulted in a balkanized campus where students did not develop positive relationships across race, these perceptions should be a serious concern for Michigan. But, as already indicated, this did not occur at Michigan, and friendships across race actually increased at Michigan over the four years.

Finally, if perception of racial tension is viewed as something to be avoided at all costs, what is the answer? Is it to return to segregated schools? It is easy for people to imagine that racial tension did not exist before affirmative action, and further that racial tension would simply disappear now, with no consequences to society, if diverse groups of Americans did not work and live closely together, and if affirmative action were not instrumental in bringing diverse groups together in our nation's most selective educational institutions.

The amicus brief submitted on behalf of the university in the affirmative action cases by former military generals and admirals challenges that point of view. Although the armed forces became integrated in 1948, there was great disparity in numbers between the officer and enlisted corps up to and through the Vietnam War.

The military amici curiae stress how negative that disparity was for the military's capacity to wage the Vietnam War.

They state that the small percentage of officers of color "and the discrimination perceived to be its cause led to low morale and heightened racial tension. The danger that this created was not theoretical, as the Vietnam era demonstrates. As that war continued, the armed forces suffered increased racial polarization, pervasive disciplinary problems, and racially motivated incidents in Vietnam and on posts around the world. . . . The military's leadership 'recognized that its racial problem was so critical that it was on the verge of self-destruction.'" (Brief of Amici Curiae Lt. Gen. Julius W. Becton, Jr., et al. at 6–7, *Grutter* [No. 02–241, 6–7].)

The example of the military demonstrates that ignoring racial issues, however harmonious race relationships might have appeared to be until the military faced a major crisis such as the Vietnam War, actually produced profound racial tension and polarization. Affirmative action that was undertaken in the armed forces academies and in ROTC following the Vietnam War has resulted in a larger proportion of officers of color and a much more realistic, healthy state of affairs. Something is clearly awry when some Americans long for the days when racial tension was not perceived but nonetheless was felt—at least by Americans of color—and largely ignored.

Societies all around the world are being threatened by racial and ethnic cleavages. Surely, college students today need to learn how to work, live, and be leaders in a diverse society lest our own heterogeneous society and democracy become as hopelessly divided as many are in the world today.

Does racial/ethnic diversity foster diversity of ideas and viewpoints? Isn't a focus on racial/ethnic diversity encouraging racial/ethnic stereotypes?

One argument that many critics of affirmative action have made against the diversity rationale has been to deny that the presence of multiple and different racial/ethnic groups on campus actually brings multiple and diverse viewpoints and perspectives to the college environment. The argument that there are no race-related differences in ideas is most strikingly evident in the opinion given by two of the three-person panel of the Fifth Circuit Court in the Hopwood case: "the use of race, in and of itself, to choose students simply achieves a student body that looks different. Such a criterion is no more rational on its own terms than would be choices based upon the physical size or blood types of individuals" (*Hopwood v. University of Texas*, 78 F.3d 932 (5th Cir. 1996), cert. Denied, 518 U.S. 1033, 950).

This argument is often buttressed by a moralistic criticism of the proponents of diversity (and of affirmative action to achieve diversity) who claim that race and ethnicity are related to intellectual points of view. Critics of affirmative action argue that to say that racial groups differ in viewpoints is to stereotype such groups.

Wood and Sherman (2001) illustrate this two-pronged argument, namely that (1) race does not provide significant viewpoint diversity, and (2) race-conscious policies invidiously stereotype minority groups. Commenting on all the cultural, social, and technological forces that they feel have fostered the homogenization of our nation and muted the significance of regional, class, and other societal divisions, Wood and Sherman conclude that "all these factors greatly diminish the impact that racial diversity will have on the intellectual, cultural, and social diversity of the student body. The same historical and social forces have also made it much more difficult . . . for universities to engage in racial stereotyping. . . . Presumably, Powell believed that racial diversity could serve to some extent as a proxy for viewpoint diversity. But it can do so only to the extent that different races have stereotypically different viewpoints" (132–33).

It is ironic and disingenuous for critics of affirmative action to charge the university with promoting group stereotypes when we argue that positive interracial experiences promote an appreciation of *both* differences and commonalities between members of different racial and ethnic groups. Our research is part of a fifty-year tradition of social psychological theory and research on interracial contact, a body of work that has demonstrated that positive and equal interracial contacts serve to diminish stereotypical thinking. In the standard definition in the literature, "stereotypes are beliefs about the characteristics, attributes, and behaviors of members of certain groups" (Hilton and von Hippel 1996, 240). While stereotypes can be positive, the focus in the literature has been on negative group stereotypes, and on the relationship between these stereotypes and prejudice and discrimination. In assigning negative characteristics to an out-group, stereotypes tend to be overly generalized and simplistic and to ignore the individual variability of members of out-groups. Instead, stereotypes exaggerate the homogeneity of out-group members. Positive, equal contact with members of an out-group serves to challenge the negativity, simplicity, overgeneralization, and homogeneity that are the essence of anti-group stereotypes.

In charging that those who support affirmative action foster racial stereotypes, Wood and Sherman are well aware that research at the University of Michigan is part of a tradition that argues just the opposite. What they claim is that it is inconsistent to say that interracial contact reduces group stereotyping and also argue that this contact produces an understanding of different group perspectives. In their words, we "can't have it both ways" (Wood and Sherman 2001, 133).

Contrary to their beliefs, positive intergroup relations foster recognition of different perspectives held by racial groups, *and* produce a more complex and nuanced view of members of one's own group(s) and of the members of other groups. It is not inconsistent to say that this complexity involves an understanding of both the different perspectives that come from the different life experiences of racial and ethnic groups in the United States, and the similarities between groups that reflect their many shared experiences. This complexity further involves an appreciation of the individual variability of members of both one's own and other racial/ethnic groups. We learn how we differ in ways we had not thought about, and we learn how we are similar in ways we had previously stereotypically assumed groups are different.

The charge that we are fostering stereotypic thinking about groups when we talk of groups having different viewpoints and perspectives ignores the fact that the different group perspectives we (and others) refer to are completely unrelated to the types of group differences that typically comprise the stereotypic views of minority groups in our society. The different perspectives that we contend students learn about from meaningful interracial experiences are those that are shaped by the experiences and histories of different racial/ethnic groups in our society. These different perspectives pertain to perceptions of our society, the individual's relation to society, evaluations of the equity in our society and in various institutions (the courts, police, educational system, economic and political institutions), and the systemic supports and barriers that shape our individual lives and affect the role of individual effort for success and failure. Encountering these differences in viewpoint has a special meaning when they come from students of different backgrounds and life experiences. What students learn from each other is not only that different viewpoints on these matters exist but also that some of the basic cultural assumptions in our society—assumptions that individuals often take as givens and are not questioned—are not such obvious truths after all but are affected by varied backgrounds, social experiences, and positions in society. These varied experiences are what make interracial relationships an impetus for learning about others and for examining and learning about oneself.

These differences in views about society are completely distinct in character from the assumed group differences that are generally thought to comprise stereotypes of groups. Group stereotypes are usually negative, and they ascribe characteristics or traits to members of other groups that serve to distance "them" from "us." When applied to groups that possess lower power, status, and resources in our society, stereotypes serve to justify inequality by attributing it to defects in the personal and value characteristics and traits of the members of the lower power/status groups rather than to structured arrangements in the social system that perpetuate inequality (Jost and Banaji 1994; Bobo 2001). This has been strikingly documented with respect to the crude stereotypes of African Americans that have been prevalent in our culture throughout our history.

It is, therefore, neither inconsistent nor surprising that proponents of diversity have always argued that the increased understanding of other groups that comes from positive interracial interactions involves appreciation of *both* the differences that emanate from different life experiences *and* the commonalities that previously stereotypes had treated as different.

These differences and commonalities are illustrated in a number of findings from the Michigan Student Study. In a particularly striking example of differences, the MSS found that students of different racial/ethnic backgrounds, especially African American and white students, differ greatly in their responses to a number of questions that tap their views of the *equity* of societal arrangements in the United States. This is evident in their views of the current state of racial justice in our nation. While a majority of all Michigan students felt that some racial discrimination and inequality still exist in our society, the racial/ethnic groups differ greatly in the strength and urgency of their conviction about this. For example, 84 percent of African American students, in contrast to only 28 percent of white students, strongly disagreed with the statement that "Most people of color are no longer discriminated against in this country."

These group differences in the perception of societal inequality extend beyond issues that focus directly on race to more general questions about the distribution of resources and rewards in our society. Students of color, particularly African American students, more often attribute income inequalities to societal rather than individual causes. For example, in a question addressing causes of wealth and poverty in the United States, 65 percent of African American students but only 20 percent of white students said that "failure of private industry to provide enough jobs" was a "very important" reason for "why there are poor people in the United States."

In contrast to these striking racial/ethnic differences in students' views of the equity of our society, the Michigan Student Study found that racial/ethnic differences were not evident in a number of arenas where prevalent stereotypes would normally predict that they would exist. Notably, the MSS data do *not* support the stereotype that underrepresented students of color, particularly African American students, do not share the core intellectual and academic values of our elite universities, and are more oriented to college for vocational and social reasons. In response to a question that asked the entering students what important experiences they hoped to have in college, African American students more often than white students chose "being a top student academically" as important, and less often chose "dating and having an active social life." The study findings also did not support another prominent component of the stereotype that underrepresented students lack academic investment, namely, that they do not accept responsibility for their academic performance and instead avoid and externalize problems when they exist. In response to the senior survey, when compared with white students, all students of color were more, not less, self-critical of their academic effort. Their greater self-criticism existed even though they reported spending just as much time on homework. These findings suggest that students of color face special pressures to prove themselves academically and that these pressures are internalized. These and other student responses discredit the stereotype of underrepresented minority students as being antiacademic, a stereotype that has been especially insidious because it serves to devalue these students and undermine the legitimacy of their presence at universities like the University of Michigan.

The MSS findings dramatize the irony of the criticism of opponents of affirmative action that we are fostering group stereotypes through our claim that a racially/ethnically diverse student body provides a wider range of ideas and perspectives. In the years since affirmative action opened our selective universities to students of color more than a generation ago, opponents of affirmative action, not the supporters, have focused on the "differences" that these students bring to the university. They have pointed not to positive or even nonevaluative differences but to stereotypically negative differences that the MSS data simply do not substantiate. Most prominent among these "differences" is the claim that African American students are anti-intellectual and not invested academically (D'Souza 1995; McWhorter 2000), and that they do not "belong" in elite universities. It is difficult to accept the sincerity of our critics' concern that stereotyping results from the efforts of selective universities to enroll a diverse student body when it has been the opponents of affirmative action who have advanced the most pernicious negative stereotypes of minority students.

Who cares about the impact of college on its students during the time they are in college? Are there any long-term effects of attending racially/ethnically diverse colleges and of having diversity experiences during college?

Despite the increasing centrality of college in preparing people for their various roles in society, college is still often viewed as a hiatus from the "real world," where students and faculty are intentionally separated by their position within the ivory tower of academia. This perspective often leads people to question whether what happens to students during college will have any long-term impact since the experiences (and changes related to these experiences) may not have any applicability once students "return" to the real world.

The limited research literature that has followed college students into the postcollege world suggests that, in fact, changes during college can have a lifelong impact on the way students live their postcollege lives. Studies such as those of the Bennington College students conducted by Newcomb and his colleagues suggest that students do in fact retain the changes that the collegiate experience has helped to create, in part due to a phenomenon of channeling, in which graduates seek out and develop postcollege environments that serve to reinforce the lessons they learned during college (Newcomb et al. 1967).

The CIRP study that formed the national component of our research provides us with the opportunity to look at whether these phenomena occur with respect to the impact of diversity. In addition to surveys of students at college entrance and four years later, the study participants were contacted again nine years after entering college. While these individuals will continue to change and develop as they grow older, this information provides important insight into whether or not collegiate changes have some permanence, while establishing the potential for long-term stability.

The pattern of results from our analyses of the nine-year data shows that the effect of college diversity experience was still statistically significant on both learning and democracy outcomes measured after students had left college. The effect of college experience with diversity was strongest on democracy outcomes. Nine years after college entry, students who had the greatest experience with diversity in college were the most likely to be engaged in volunteering in community service; to value volunteering in the community as a chance "to work with people different from me," "to influence society as a whole," "to improve my community," and "to fulfill my social responsibility." They also placed the most importance on "influencing the political structure," "influencing social values," "helping others in difficulty," "being involved in programs to clean up the environment," and "participating in a community action program" (citizenship engagement). They were the most likely to say that they had increased their "cultural awareness and appreciation" and "acceptance of persons from different races and cultures" (racial/cultural engagement). And finally they were most likely to have diverse "current close friends," diverse "current neighbors," and diverse "current work associates" (living in a diverse society). Since this immediate postcollege period is critical in establishing a trajectory for the future lives of these students, we would expect the effects of college diversity on sentiments necessary for citizenship in a diverse democracy to be maintained over the long run.

The impact of diversity experience during college on the greater likelihood of having diverse friends, neighbors, and coworkers is especially noteworthy since social scientists have documented that racial isolation and segregation tend to be perpetuated over the stages of the life cycle and across institutional settings. Majority and minority individuals whose childhood experiences take place in schools and neighborhoods that are largely segregated are likely to lead their adult lives in similarly segregated occupational and residential settings (Braddock, Dawkins, and Trent 1994; Braddock and McPartland 1987; Braddock and McPartland 1988). College is a uniquely opportune time to disrupt this pattern. Moreover, we know that previously segregated minority students who attend diverse colleges and universities are the most likely to find themselves in desegregated employment and to work in professional jobs in the private sectors. Wells and Crain (1994) suggest that the networking students are able to do in diverse colleges and universities is an important explanation for later employment in racially/ethnically diverse work settings. Our findings from the national study on the impact of diversity experience in college on living in a diverse society show that at the critical time of late adolescence and early adulthood, college students have an opportunity to disrupt an insidious cycle of lifetime segregation that threatens the fabric of our pluralistic democracy.

Is it really the business of colleges and universities to prepare students to be citizens and leaders in politics, government and the military, corporations, and communities?

Some critics have argued that what we have referred to as democracy outcomes are not relevant educational goals and instead are examples of "political correctness." As we have noted, this criticism reflects an ignorance of the centrality of such outcomes in the history of higher education in the United States.

From the founding of public higher education institutions in the first quarter of the 1800s, and certainly since the time of Thomas Jefferson, who felt that citizens must be created through education and who made the founding of the University of Virginia the primary work of his postpresidential years, a central mission of universities has been to produce educated citizens and leaders for our democracy.

Political scientist Benjamin Barber stresses that all traditional political theories—liberal, republican, and democratic—have viewed citizens as created, not born. He asks the question: "Does a university have a civic mission? Of course, for it *is* a civic mission. The cultivation of free community—of civility itself" (Barber 1998, 182).

But how does diversity foster civic preparedness? It plays a role in two critically important theories that we drew upon in the theoretical rationale laid out in the early part of this chapter: Aristotle's theory of democracy that is built on difference rather than on similarity, and Piaget's theory of moral development that emphasizes discussion by peers of discrepant, often conflicting, points of view. They emphasize the following conditions for democracy and moral reasoning: the presence of diverse others, who bring multiple, and sometimes conflicting, perspectives; discussion among peers who are equals; and discussion under rules of civil discourse.

These conditions are what racial/ethnic diversity brings to students at the University of Michigan, providing that administrators and faculty assure that students from different racial and ethnic backgrounds interact with each other and discuss under rules of civil discourse the many perspectives that arise from their different life experiences. Educators have an important role to play, not by telling students what to believe, as the charge of "political correct-

ness" implies, but by creating an environment where racial diversity can lead to the very conditions both Aristotle and Piaget believed were crucial for a democracy and for moral development.

Higher education must prepare students today to be leaders in an incredibly and increasingly diverse society. This is the mission of the University of Michigan both for undergraduate students and for law students. Law in particular is a public profession that is tied up with all aspects of the public world. The University of Michigan has an obligation to educate undergraduates to be citizens and leaders in the broad arenas in which they will work and live, and to train lawyers for leadership positions in both the private and public sectors.

This is exactly why a wide range and impressively large number of organizations in the United States joined together to support the university's cases at the Supreme Court. More than seventy-five amicus briefs were submitted representing hundreds of colleges and universities; more than fifty higher education associations representing virtually every college and university in the nation; sixty-eight Fortune 500 corporations; twenty-nine former high-ranking military leaders; twenty-four U.S. states and territories; labor unions; religious organizations (including the American Jewish Committee, which was opposed to affirmative action at the time of the *Bakke* case); more than two dozen members of Congress; the major social science organizations within education, sociology, and psychology (the American Education Research Association, the American Psychological Association, the American Sociological Association); civil rights organizations (the NAACP Legal Defense Fund, the Leadership Conference on Civil Rights, the National Urban League, the United Negro College Fund, and the ACLU); a dozen Native American tribes and organizations; twenty-five Asian/Pacific-American organizations; Hispanic and Latino organizations (including the New American Alliance); the National Academy of Sciences and National Academy of Engineering; twenty-eight broadcast media companies and organizations; legal organizations and legal education groups (including the American Bar Association); more than fourteen thousand law students nationwide; and the authors of the 10 percent admissions plan in Texas.[11]

What did all of these organizations that represented the mainstream of American institutional life have in common? All of them argued, in different ways reflecting their different institutional perspectives, that racial and ethnic diversity at the nation's most selective institutions is essential for producing members and leaders of their organizations who know how to deal with diverse constituencies and clients. They argue, further, that the health, vibrancy, and security of our democracy are at stake.

General Motors Corporation, which previously had submitted an amicus brief at the district court on behalf of the university, argues in its brief to the Supreme Court that the increasingly global and interconnected nature of the world economy and the increasingly diverse population of the United States set up a business environment that requires culturally competent business leaders.

> To succeed in this increasingly diverse environment, American businesses must select leaders who possess cross-cultural competence—the capacities to interact with and to understand the experiences of, and multiplicity of perspectives held by, persons of different races, ethnicities and cultural histories. . . . Much research confirms what is intuitively obvious: students are likely to acquire greater cross-cultural competence in a multicultural and multiracial academic environment, in which students and faculty of different cultures and races interact, than they are in a homogeneous one, in which cross-cultural communication is merely a theoretical construct. (Brief of Amici Curiae General Motors Corporation at 8, *Grutter*, No. 02–241, 4)

Brief after brief submitted on behalf of the University of Michigan makes similar claims. These mainstream organizations look to higher education to prepare students to be future leaders of our pluralistic, indeed increasingly heterogeneous, democracy and of our major economic and other societal institutions. These organizations know, as society is now constructed with widespread neighborhood and K–12 school segregation, that it is only in higher education institutions that students of all racial/ethnic backgrounds can gain the experiences and skills that are so much needed for the United States to be a viable and trusted leader nation in the world and for organizations and institutions within the United States to function effectively, competitively, and compassionately.

Conclusion

We have documented a consistent picture from both our research and the research of other scholars that shows a wide range of educational benefits when students interact and learn from each other across race and ethnicity. The amicus briefs on behalf of the plaintiffs mention only a few studies indicating possible negative effects of affirmative action, none of which focus on important educational outcomes for students. Instead, they have focused on critiquing the research conducted to support the educational benefits of diversity, though their critiques do not mention either the confirmatory research that we covered in our expert testimony or the research conducted by many others that has been brought forward since we submitted our testimony to the district court. They are silent on the impressive amount of research cited in the educational, psychological, and sociological amicus briefs supporting the benefits of racial/ethnic diversity.

Still, a question could be raised about the overwhelmingly positive picture that we have painted in this chapter. Are there no negative student reactions to the University of Michigan's emphasis on what was earlier termed the Michigan Mandate and is now thought of as simply its emphasis on diversity? Of course, some students criticize these institutional emphases. We have already recounted that this is true, but we emphasize that the percentage of students who actually hold negative views of their *own intergroup experiences* is very small.

There are many challenges ahead. First of all, only about 50 to 60 percent of the students had the classroom and informal interactions with diverse peers that we have shown produced positive student outcomes. It is possible—indeed easy—for students to remain in homogeneous groupings on the campus, often replicating their home environments in fraternities and sororities and in other social settings. When students stay in what they call their "comfort zones," they are shortchanging what a Michigan education can offer to them. But to fully maximize the potential of a diverse student body, the University of Michigan must continue to offer curricular and cocurricular opportunities for students to interact with each other, and especially to interact over a sustained period of time in environments that foster the personal, sharing relationships that account for positive outcomes for students. The residence halls, in particular, should be such settings, since nearly all incoming first-year students live in the residence halls.

For most of Michigan's students, its residence halls are the most diverse environments they have ever encountered. Students live with each other over an extended time. Rooming with a student from a different racial/ethnic background, though sometimes a genuine challenge for these previously racially segregated students, is potentially a very positive experience. We have seen from the experiment conducted by Duncan and colleagues (2003) that cross-racial roommate experiences had important benefits for students. Universities also need to enhance the capacities of faculty who are interested in using student diversity for maximal learning. Such faculty benefit from support and opportunities to share best practices and ways of handling problems that inevitably arise when different, even conflicting, perspectives and emotion are allowed, indeed encouraged, in classroom discussion. Programs, such as the Program on Intergroup Relations, that provide safe places for students to "go beyond their comfort zones"—taking risks to deal with the difficult issue of race in America—need to be sustained and promoted. This specific program has in fact been adopted at numerous universities around the country. These educational opportunities, and many more, must be nourished *and* evaluated.

Second, the University of Michigan faces complexities in how various groups of students interpret the meaning of diversity and multicultural education. For students of color the university's commitment to diversity not only provides the opportunity to interact with and learn from students of other backgrounds and cultures but also gives legitimacy to the unique experiences and cultural contributions of their own groups. Until recently these experiences and contributions have been mostly excluded from the intellectual and social life of our college campuses. Students of color, particularly African American students, have responded to this recognition of the uniqueness of different group experiences in two ways: learning more about their own groups' histories and their own identities, and learning more about other groups. This is also true of white students, but many fewer of them than seniors of color, especially African American seniors, say that they "gained a greater commitment to their racial/ethnic group since coming to the University," and that they "gained greater knowledge of their groups' contributions to American society." For white students the university's commitment to diversity brings more ambivalent reactions. While most white students support the principles of cultural pluralism and have reacted positively to their own diversity experiences at Michigan, many of them are also concerned that too much focus on group differences may constrain the ability of white students and students of color to relate to each other "as individuals." Three times as many white seniors as African American seniors, for example, agreed that "the University's focus on diversity puts too much emphasis on differences." These reactions reflect the complexity of simultaneously acknowledging the existence of groups *and* individuals that is central to the national debate on diversity. A related aspect of this complexity comes from the great intergroup differences the Michigan Student Study has documented, particularly between African American and white students, on questions that tap students' views of racial discrimination and racial justice, as well as their ideas about what should be done about these issues. These differences mirror equally large differences between whites and African Americans in national surveys of the adult population in the United States (Bobo 2001). We have stressed that these different perspectives on the fault line of race in America are a critical aspect of the value of diversity and an impetus for growth in understanding and self-exploration. But they can also create barriers to intergroup communication unless exploration of differences is conducted under clear rules of civil discourse. While complex, this university and other universities must continually offer students such a civil society—safe places for genuine discussion and sharing of personal experiences across race—in which they can grapple with the contested meanings of diversity, democracy, equity, justice, difference and commonality, and community. Anything less fails to use the institutional resource that a diverse student body represents.

Third, as the University of Michigan looks to the future, a major recommendation to create greater public understanding and support for affirmative action made by Faye Crosby (2004) is of the utmost importance. The university must engage with its various constituencies about diversity and affirmative action. In the early days of using race-conscious policies in admission before the onset of the litigation, the university may not have provided sufficient information to the student body and to the wider public about the qualifications of the students of color who are admitted to the university. We perhaps erred in not explaining to more potentially interested audiences how affirmative action actually worked at the University of Michigan or why it benefited all students by assuring a diverse study body in its undergraduate and graduate schools. In hindsight we perhaps unwittingly fostered an invalid suspicion of our admission policies. Although suspicion and resentment are problems that the Supreme Court decision may have somewhat ameliorated, we must continue to be mindful of the importance of helping our students, faculty, staff, and the wider public understand what our new undergraduate policy is, how it assures admitting absolutely qualified students, how it addresses the guidance of the Supreme Court, and why affirmative action continues to be necessary into the foreseeable future to assure racial and ethnic diversity at the University of Michigan.

Finally, we reflect back on the journey that we took in providing a rationale for the educational value of diversity, using data available to us in 1998, and examining the research of other scholars that had been published at that time. The critical question for us then and now is the impact of social science research on the Court. Did our research and the research of other social scientists, summarized by various amicus briefs on behalf of the University of Michigan, have a significant impact on the Court? The answer to that question, of course, lies in the deliberations within the Court about which we can only guess. We believe that Michigan's defense of its admission policies to achieve racial/ethnic diversity was greatly strengthened by social science evidence. All of the court cases involving affirmative action in higher education previously had depended nearly exclusively on anecdotal evidence. We also believe that Michigan's defense was enormously enhanced by the arguments brought forward by the large number of mainstream organizations and institutions as amici curiae for the university. Their arguments were fashioned both from their own experiences and from the student outcomes that we and others had delineated as the consequences of having curricular and cocurricular experiences with diversity. The synergy between the research and these multiple arguments made by corporations, the military, higher education, labor unions, and many other organizations clearly helped what was already a strong defense put together by the university and its lawyers. As we look back, we feel honored and gratified to have been part of the process.

REFERENCES

Acredolo, C., and J. O'Connor. 1991. "On the Difficulty of Detecting Cognitive Uncertainty." *Human Development* 34:204–23.

Allport, G. 1954. *The Nature of Prejudice.* Cambridge, Mass.: Addison-Wesley.

Alwin, D. F., R. I. Cohen, and T. M. Newcomb. 1991. *Political Attitudes over the Life Span.* Madison: University of Wisconsin Press.

Amir, Y. 1976. "The Role of Intergroup Contact in the Change of Prejudice and Ethnic Relations." In *Towards the Elimination of Racism,* ed. P. A. Katz, 245–308. New York: Pergamon Press.

Antonio, A. 1998. "The Impact of Friendship Groups in a Multicultural University." Ph.D. diss., University of California, Los Angeles.

———. 2001. "The Role of Interracial Interaction in the Development of Leadership Skills and Cultural Knowledge and Understanding." *Research in Higher Education* 42:593–617.

Aron, A., E. N. Aron, and D. Smollen. 1992. "Inclusion of Other in the Self Scale and the Structure of Interpersonal Closeness." *Journal of Personality and Social Psychology* 63:596–612.

Aron, A., E. N. Aron, M. Tudor, and G. Nelson. 1991. "Close Relationships as Including Other in the Self." *Journal of Personality and Social Psychology* 60:241–53.

Aron, A., E. Melinat, E. N. Aron, R. Vallone, and R. Bator. 1997. "The Experimental Generation of Interpersonal Closeness: A Procedure and Some Preliminary Findings." *Personality and Social Psychology Bulletin* 23:363–77.

Barber, B. R. 1989. "Public Talk and Civic Action: Education for Participation in a Strong Democracy." *Social Education* (October) 355–56, 370.

———. 1998. *A Passion for Democracy.* Princeton: Princeton University Press.

Bargh, J. A. 1997. "The Automaticity of Everyday Life." *Advances in Social Cognition* 10:2–48.

Berlyne, D. E. 1970. "Children's Reasoning and Thinking." In *Carmichael's Manual of Child Psychology,* ed. P. H. Mussen, 1:939–81. New York: Wiley.

Blair, I. V. 2002. "The Malleability of Automatic Stereotypes and Prejudice." *Personality and Social Psychology Review* 6, no. 3: 242–61.

Blascovich, J., N. Wyer, L. Swart, and J. L. Kibler. 1997. "Racism and Racial Categorization." *Journal of Personality and Social Psychology* 72:1364–72.

Bobo, L. D. 2001. "Racial Attitudes and Relations at the Close of the Twentieth Century." In *America Becoming: Racial Trends and Their Consequences,* ed. N. J. Smelser, W. J. Wilson, and F. Mitchell, 1:264–301. Washington, D.C.: National Academy Press.

Bobo, L. D., and D. Johnson. 2000. "Racial Attitudes in a Prismatic Metropolis: Mapping Identity, Stereotypes, Competition, and Views on Affirmative Action." In *Prismatic Metropolis,* ed. L. D. Bobo, M. L. Oliver, J. H. Johnson Jr., and A. Valenzuela Jr., 81–166. New York: Russell Sage Foundation.

Bowen, W. G. 1977. "Admissions and the Relevance of Race." *Princeton Alumni Weekly,* September 26, 1977, 7, 9.

Bowen, W. G., and D. Bok. 1998. *The Shape of the River: Long-Term Consequences of Considering Race in College and University Admissions.* Princeton: Princeton University Press.

Braddock, J. H., M. P. Dawkins, and W. Trent. 1994. "Why Desegregate? The Effect of School Desegregation on Adult Occupational Desegregation of African Americans, Whites, and Hispanics." *International Journal of Contemporary Sociology* 31, no. 2: 273–83.

Braddock, J. H., and J. M. McPartland. 1987. "How Minorities Continue to Be Excluded from Equal Employment Opportunities: Research on Labor Market and Institutional Barriers." *Journal of Social Issues* 43:5–39.

———. 1988. "The Social and Academic Consequences of School Desegregation." *Equity and Choice* 5:63–73.

Brief of the American Psychological Association as *Amici Curiae* in Support of Respondents. *Grutter v. Bollinger et al.,* No. 02–241 (2003); *Gratz v. Bollinger et al.,* No. 02–516 (2003).

Brief of General Motors Corporation as *Amici Curiae* in Support of Respondents. *Grutter v. Bollinger et al.,* No. 02–241 (2003); *Gratz v. Bollinger et al.,* No. 02–516 (2003).

Brief of Lt. Gen. Julius W. Becton, Jr., et al. as *Amici Curiae* in support of Respondents. *Grutter v. Bollinger et al.,* No. 02–241.

Brief of the National Association of Scholars as *Amici Curiae* in Support of Petitioners. *Gratz v. Bollinger et al.,* No. 02–516 (2003).

Brief of the National Education Association, et al. as *Amici Curiae* in Support of Respondents. *Grutter v. Bollinger et al.,* No. 02–241 (2003); *Gratz v. Bollinger et al.,* No. 02–516 (2003).

Carter, S. 1991. *Reflection of an Affirmative Action Baby.* New York: Basic Books.

Chang, M. J. 1996. "Racial Diversity in Higher Education: Does a Racially Mixed Student Population Affect Educational Outcomes?" Ph.D. diss., University of California, Los Angeles.

———. 1999. "Does Racial Diversity Matter? The Educational Impact of a Racially Diverse Undergraduate Population." *Journal of College Student Development* 40:377–95.

Chang, M. J., A. W. Astin, and D. Kim. 2004. "Cross-Racial Interaction among Undergraduates: Some Causes and Consequences." *Research in Higher Education.*

Chang, M. J., K. Hakuta, and J. Jones. 2002. *Compelling Interest: Examining the Evidence on Racial Dynamics in Colleges and Universities.* Palo Alto, Calif.: Stanford University Press.

Chang, M. J., M. Seltzer, and J. Kim. 2002. "Diversity of Opinions among Entering College Students: Does Race Matter?" Research paper presented at the National Academy of Education Annual Meeting, Toronto, Canada, October.

Cook, S. W. 1984. "Cooperative Interaction in Multiethnic Contexts." In *Groups in Contact: The Psychology of Desegregation,* ed. N. Miller and M. B. Brewer, 154–85. New York: Academic Press.

Crosby, F. 2004. *Affirmative Action Is Dead; Long Live Affirmative Action.* New Haven: Yale University Press.

D'Souza, D. 1995. *The End of Racism: Principles for a Multiracial Society.* New York: Free Press.

Devine, P. G. 1989. "Stereotypes and Prejudice: Their Automatic and Controlled Components." *Journal of Personality and Social Psychology* 56:5–18.

Doise, W., and A. Palmonari, eds. 1984. *Social Interaction in Individual Development.* Cambridge: Cambridge University Press.

Dovidio J. F., and S. L. Gaertner. 2000. "Aversive Racism and Selection Decisions: 1989 and 1999." *Psychological Science* 11:315–19.

Dovidio, J., K. Kawakami, and S. L. Gaertner. 2002. "Implicit and Explicit

Prejudice and Interracial Interactions." *Journal of Personality and Social Psychology* 82:62–68.

Dovidio, J. F., K. Kawakami, C. Johnson, B. Johnson, and A. Howard. 1997. "On the Nature of Prejudice: Automatic and Controlled Processes." *Journal of Experimental Social Psychology* 33:510–40.

Downing, R., M. E. Lubensky, S. Sincaharoen, P. Gurin, F. J. Crosby, S. Quierolo, and J. Franco. 2002. "Affirmative Action in Higher Education." *Diversity Factor* 10, no. 2: 15–20.

Duncan, G. J., J. Boisjoly, D. M. Levy, M. Kremer, and J. Eccles. 2003. "Empathy or Antipathy? The Consequences of Racially and Socially Diverse Peers on Attitudes and Behaviors." Accessed June 1, 2003. Available at http://www.jcpr.org/wp/Wpprofile.cfm?ID=384.

Erikson, E. 1946. "Ego Development and Historical Change." *Psychoanalytic Study of the Child* 2:359–96.

———. 1956. "The Problem of Ego Identity." *Journal of the American Psychoanalytic Association* 4:56–121.

Fazio, R. H., and M. A. Olson. 2003. "Implicit Measures in Social Cognition Research: Their Meaning and Use." *Annual Review of Psychology* 54:297, 306, 310.

Flanagan, C. A., and L. R. Sherrod. 1998. "Youth Political Movement: An Introduction." *Journal of Social Issues* 54:447–56.

Flanagan, C. A., and C. J. Tucker. 1999. "Adolescents' Explanation for Political Issues: Concordance with Their Views of Self and Society." *Developmental Psychology* 35:1198–1209.

Fredrickson, G. M. 1999. "Models of American Ethnic Relations: A Historical Perspective." In *Cultural Divides: The Social Psychology of Intergroup Contact,* ed. D. Prentice and D. Miller. New York: Russell Sage Foundation.

Genova, W. J., and H. J. Walberg. 1980. "Practitioners' Guide for Achieving Student Integration in City High Schools." ERIC Document ED200669.

Guarasci, R., and G. H. Cornwell, eds. 1997. *Democratic Education in an Age of Difference: Redefining Citizenship in Higher Education.* San Francisco: Jossey-Bass.

Gurin, P. 2001. "Evidence for the Educational Benefits of Diversity in Higher Education: Response to the Wood and Sherman Critique by the National Association of Scholars of the Expert Witness Report of Patricia Gurin in *Gratz, et al. v Bollinger, et al.* and *Grutter v Bollinger, et al.*" Available at http://www.umich.edu/~urel/admissions/research/gurin.html.

———. 2003. "Evidence for the Educational Benefits of Diversity in Higher

Education: Response to the Continuing Critique by the National Association of Scholars of the Expert Witness Report of Patricia Gurin in *Gratz, et al. v Bollinger, et al.* and *Grutter v Bollinger, et al.*" Available at http://www.umich.edu/~urel/admissions/research/pgurin-nas.html.

Gurin, P., E. L. Dey, S. Hurtado, and G. Gurin. 2002. "Diversity and Higher Education: Theory and Impact on Educational Outcomes." *Harvard Educational Review* 72, no. 3: 330–66.

Gurin, P., G. Gurin, and J. Matlock. 2003. "Response to Diversity Distorted: How the University of Michigan Withheld Data to Hide Evidence of Racial Conflict and Polarization by Robert Lerner and Althea K. Nagai." Available at http://www.umich.edu/~urel/admissions/research/pgurin-ln.html.

Gurin, P., B. Nagda, and G. Lopez. 2004. "Preparation for Citizenship." *Journal of Social Issues.*

Hilton, J. L., and W. Von Hippel. 1996. "Stereotypes." *Annual Review of Psychology* 47:237–71.

Hurtado, S. 2001. "Linking Diversity with Educational Purpose: How Diversity Impacts the Classroom Environment and Student Development." In *Diversity Challenged: Legal Crisis and New Evidence,* ed. G. Orfield. Cambridge: Harvard Publishing Group.

Hurtado, S., E. L. Dey, and J. G. Trevino. 1994. "Exclusion or Self-Segregation? Interaction across Racial/Ethnic Groups on Campus." Paper presented at the Annual Meeting of the American Educational Research Association, New Orleans.

Jackman, M. R., and M. J. Muha. 1984. "Education and Intergroup Attitudes: Moral Enlightenment, Superficial Democratic Commitment, or Ideological Refinement?" *American Sociological Review* 49:751–69.

Jost, J. T., and M. R. Banaji. 1994. "The Role of Stereotyping in System-Justification and the Production of False Consciousness." *British Journal of Social Psychology* 33:1–28.

Jost, J. T., and B. Major. 2001. *The Psychology of Legitimacy: Emerging Perspectives on Ideology, Justice, and Intergroup Relations.* Cambridge: Cambridge University Press.

Kolb, D. A. 1984. *Experiential Learning: Experience as the Source of Learning and Development.* New York: Prentice-Hall.

Kuh, G. D. 2003. "What We're Learning about Student Engagement from NSSE." *Change* 35, no. 2: 24.

Langer, E. J. 1978. "Rethinking the Role of Thought in Social Interaction." In *New Directions in Attribution Research,* ed. J. Harvey, W. Ickes, and R. Kiss, 3:35–38. Hillsdale, N.J.: Lawrence Erlbaum Associates.

Lerner, R., and A. Nagai. 2001. "A Critique of the Expert Report of Patricia Gurin in Gratz v. Bollinger." Available at: http://www.ceousa.org/new2.html.

———. 2003. "Diversity Distorted: How the University of Michigan Withheld Data to Hide Evidence of Racial Conflict and Polarization." Available at http://www.ceousa.org/pdfs/hiddendata.pdf.

Lopez, G. E., P. Gurin, and B. A. Nagda. 1998. "Education and Understanding Structural Causes for Group Inequalities." *Journal of Political Psychology* 19, no. 2: 305–29.

MacPhee, D., J. C. Kreutzer, and J. J. Fritz. 1994. "Infusing a Diversity Perspective into Human Development Courses." *Child Development* 65, no. 2: 699–715.

McAdams, D. P. 1988. "Personal Needs and Personal Relationships." In *Handbook of Personal Relationships: Theory, Research, and Interventions,* ed. S. W. Duck, 7–22. Chichester, UK: Wiley.

McConnell, A. R., and J. M. Liebold. 2001. "Relations among the Implicit Association Test, Discriminatory Behavior, and Explicit Measures of Racial Attitudes." *Journal of Experimental Social Psychology* 37:435–42.

McWhorter, J. 2000. *Losing the Race: Self-Sabotage in Black America.* New York: Free Press.

Milem, J. F., and K. Hakuta. 2000. "The Benefits of Racial and Ethnic Diversity in Higher Education." In *Minorities in Higher Education: Seventeenth Annual Status Report,* ed. D. Eilds, 39–67. Washington, D.C.: American Council on Education.

Mullen, B., and L. Hu. 1989. "Perceptions of Ingroup and Outgroup Variability: A Meta-analytic Integration." *Basic and Applied Social Psychology* 10:233–52.

Nagda, B. A., P. Gurin, and G. E. Lopez. 2003. "Transformative Pedagogy for Democracy and Social Justice." *Race, Ethnicity, and Education* 6, no. 2:165–91.

Newcomb, T. L., K. E. Koenig, R. Flacks, and D. P. Warwick. 1967. *Persistence and Change: Bennington College and Its Students after Twenty Years.* New York: John Wiley.

Newcomb. T. M. 1943. *Personality and Social Change: Attitude Formation in a Student Community.* New York: Dryden Press.

Orfield, G., and E. Miller, eds. 1998. *Chilling Admissions: The Affirmative Action Crisis and the Search for Alternatives.* Cambridge: Harvard Education Publishing Group and the Civil Rights Project, Harvard University.

Orfield, G., and D. Whitla. 2001. "Diversity and Legal Education: Student

Experiences in Leading Law Schools." In *Diversity Challenged: Evidence on the Impact of Affirmative Action,* ed. G. Orfield and M. Kurlaender, 143–74. Cambridge: Harvard Publishing Group.

Pascarella, E. T., M. Edison, A. Nora, L. S. Hagedorn, and P. T. Terenzini. 1996. "Influences on Students' Openness to Diversity and Challenge in the First Year of College." *Journal of Higher Education* 65, no. 2: 174–95.

Pascarella, E. T., and P. T. Terenzini. 1991. *How College Affects Students.* San Francisco: Jossey-Bass.

Pascarella, E. T., E. J. Whitt, A. Nora, M. Edison, L. S. Hagedorn, and P. T. Terenzini. 1996. "What Have We Learned from the First Year of the National Study of Student Learning?" *Journal of College Student Development* 37, no. 2: 182–92.

Pettigrew, T. 1998. "Intergroup Contact Theory." *Annual Review of Psychology* 49:65–85.

Pettigrew, T., and L. Tropp. 2000. "Does Intergroup Contact Reduce Prejudice? Recent Meta-analytic Findings." In *Reducing Prejudice and Discrimination,* ed. S. Oskamp, 93–114. Mahwah, N.J.: Lawrence Erlbaum Associates.

Piaget, J. 1971. "The Theory of Stages in Cognitive Development." In *Measurement and Piaget,* ed. D. R. Green, M. P. Ford, and G. B. Flamer, 1–11. New York: McGraw-Hill.

———. 1985. *The Equilibration of Cognitive Structures: The Central Problem of Intellectual Development.* Chicago: University of Chicago Press.

Pitkin, H. F., and S. M. Shumer. 1982. "On Participation." *Democracy* 2:43–54.

Raudenbush, S. G. 2003. "Study on Effects of Diversity Reaches Wrong Conclusions." Accessed June 1, 2003. Available at http://www.umich.edu/~urel/admissions/research/rebut-raudenbush.html.

Reis, H. T., and P. Shaver. 1988. "Intimacy as Interpersonal Process." In *Handbook of Personal Relationships: Theory, Research, and Interventions,* ed. S. W. Duck, 367–89. Chichester, UK: Wiley.

Rodriguez, R. 1981. *Hunger of Memory: The Education of Richard Rodriguez* [an autobiography]. Boston: D. R. Godine.

Rothman, S., S. M. Lipset, and N. Nevitte. 2003. "Does Enrollment Diversity Improve University Education?" *International Journal of Public Opinion Research* 15, no. 1: 8–26.

Ruble, D. 1994. "Developmental Changes in Achievement Evaluation: Motivational Implications of Self-Other Differences." *Child Development* 65:1095–1110.

Saxonhouse, A. 1992. *Fear of Diversity: The Birth of Political Science in Ancient Greek Thought.* Chicago: University of Chicago Press.

Sekaquaptewa, D., P. Espinoza, M. Thompson, P. Vargas, and W. Von Hippel. 2003. "Stereotypic Explanatory Bias: Implicit Stereotyping as a Predictor of Discrimination." *Journal of Experimental Social Psychology* 39:75.

Spencer, S. J., S. Fein, C. Wolfe, C. Fong, and M. Dunn. 1998. "Automatic Activation of Stereotypes: The Role of Self-Image Threat." *Personality and Social Psychology Bulletin* 24:1139.

Steele, S. 1990. *The Content of Our Character: A New Vision of Race in America.* New York: St. Martin's Press.

Stephan, W., and C. W. Stephan. 2001. *Improving Intergroup Relations.* Thousand Oaks, Calif.: Sage.

Sugrue, T. 1999. Expert Report, "The Compelling Need for Diversity in Higher Education." Prepared for *Gratz, et al. v. Bollinger, et al.* No. 97–75231 (E.D. Mich.) and *Grutter, et al. v. Bollinger, et al.* No. 97–75928 (E.D. Mich.).

Terenzini, P. T., L. I. Rendon, M. L. Upcraft, S. B. Millar, K. W. Allison, P. L. Gregg, and R. Jalomo. 1994. "The Transition to College: Diverse Students, Diverse Stories." *Research in Higher Education* 35, no. 1: 57–73.

Upcraft, M. L. 1989. "Understanding Student Development: Insights from Theory." In *The Freshman Year.* San Francisco: Jossey-Bass.

Vasquez-Scalera, C. 1999. "Democracy, Diversity, Dialogue: Education for Critical Multicultural Citizenship." Ph.D. diss., University of Michigan, Ann Arbor.

Von Hippel, W., D. Sekaquaptewa, and P. Vargas. 1997. "The Linguistic Intergroup Bias as an Implicit Indicator of Prejudice." *Journal of Experimental Social Psychology* 33:490.

Wells, S. A., and R. L. Crain. 1994. "Perpetuation Theory and the Long-Term Effects of School Desegregation." *Review of Educational Research* 64:531–35.

Whitla, D. K., G. Orfield, W. Silen, C. Teperow, and C. Howard. 2003. "Educational Benefits of Diversity in Medical School: A Survey of Students." *Academic Medicine* 78:460–66.

Whitt, E. J., M. J. Edison, E. T. Pascarella, P. T. Terenzini, and A. Nora. 1998. "Influences on Students' Openness to Diversity and Challenge in the Second and Third Year of College." Paper presented at the annual meeting of the Association for the Study of Higher Education, Miami.

Wood, T. E., and M. J. Sherman. 2001. "Is Campus Racial Diversity Correlated with Educational Benefits?" Accessed June 1, 2003. Available at http://nas.org/reports/umich_diversity/umich_uncorrelate.pdf.

————. 2003. "Supplement to Race and Higher Education." Accessed June 1, 2003. Available at http://nas.org/rhe2.pdf.

Yates, M., and J. Youniss, eds. 1999. *Roots of Civic Identity: International Perspectives on Community Service and Activism on Youth.* Cambridge: Cambridge University Press.

Yeakley, A. 1998. "The Nature of Prejudice Change: Positive and Negative Change Processes Arising from Intergroup Contact Experiences." Ph.D. diss., University of Michigan, Ann Arbor.

Youniss, J., J. A. McClellan, and M. Yates. 1997. "What We Know about Engendering Civic Identity." *American Behavioral Scientist* 40:620–31.

Youniss, J., and M. Yates. 1997. *Community Service and Social Responsibility in Youth: Theory and Policy.* Chicago: University of Chicago Press.

Zúñiga, X., and B. A. Nagda. 1993. "Dialogue groups: An Innovative Approach to Multicultural Learning." In *Multicultural Teaching in the University,* ed. D. Schoem, L. Frankel, X. Zúñiga, and E. Lewis, 233–48. Westport, Conn.: Praeger.

Zúñiga, X., B. A. Nagda, and T. D. Sevig. 2002. "Intergroup Dialogues: An Educational Model for Cultivating Student Engagement across Differences." *Equity and Excellence in Education* 35, no. 1: 7–17.

Afterword

Mary Sue Coleman

The decisions of the Supreme Court in the cases involving affirmative action in admissions at the University of Michigan have provided us with the guidance that higher education has been seeking for decades, namely, a well-structured road map that permits all colleges and universities to create policies of affirmative action that more clearly articulate the goals of diversity. The University of Michigan, like many other colleges and universities, began a review of current policies almost immediately following the delivery of the decisions. But the decisions do not merely chart the course for higher education—they issue a challenge to our entire nation, a challenge to create a society in which affirmative action will no longer be necessary.

The decisions of June 2003 are the latest iteration of a series of landmark decisions on education and civil rights that the Supreme Court has issued over the past fifty years. It has created large Newtonian cycles of action and reaction in the area of diversity, with three landmark decisions issued in quarter-century increments. The profound rulings on racial equality in *Brown v. Board of Education* (1954), *Regents of the University of California v. Bakke* (1978), and the University of Michigan cases have altered, and will continue to shape, the landscape of our universities and our society.

These decisions have produced phases in the evolution of our society. The decisions themselves are just the starting point for change: the policy shifts that have occurred *in between* those major decisions are what have truly transformed our nation. As of June 23, 2003, we have entered the next period of transformation that will define the history of civil rights and educational access in our country.

The Court issued a resounding reaffirmation of affirmative action as a compelling state interest, a policy that had been clearly articulated in the multitude of amicus briefs that were filed at the Supreme Court. These briefs offer vivid insight into the value of diversity to our entire society, from universities to industry to the military. While many educational institutions and organizations filed briefs on our behalf, the Court also received statements from major corporations, from nonprofit organizations, from elected officials, and from retired military leaders. It is striking to see the impact of these briefs on the thinking of the Court, and the manner in which its decisions reflect the broad concerns of many sectors of our society.

The University of Michigan made a strong case for the pedagogical benefits of diversity in campus communities and classrooms, but the amicus briefs made an equally strong case for the advantages of diversity in the workforce of our country. For example, General Motors conveyed the view that a diverse workforce is necessary not only for the sake of its own industry, but for the national and world economy:

In General Motors' experience, only a well educated, diverse work force, comprising people who have learned to work productively and creatively with individuals from a multitude of races and ethnic, religious, and cultural backgrounds, can maintain America's competitiveness in the increasingly diverse and interconnected world economy.[1]

This quest for the strength that diverse members of society can provide to an organization or community extends to cultural endeavors as well:

MTVN's [Music Television Networks'] unique mix of eclectic shows and edgy attitude was invented—and is being reinvented daily—by the most dynamic and eclectic people in the industry. This unique mix, in turn, is feeding the marketplace of ideas and shaping national and global attitudes. The future of American business and the quality of message communicated through the media "depends upon leaders trained through wide exposure to the ideas and mores" as diverse as the nation's people.[2]

One of the most striking briefs filed in support of the University of Michigan was submitted by retired military officers of the United States armed forces. Their accounts of the special situations created by the military chain of command were cited by the justices during the oral arguments of the case, and in the final Court decision in *Grutter v. Bollinger*. These former leaders of our armed forces dynamically articulated the problems they had faced because of the lack of diversity in the upper ranks of their organizations:

The chasm between the racial composition of the officer corps and the enlisted personnel undermined military effectiveness in a variety of ways. For example, military effectiveness depends heavily upon unit cohesion. In turn, group cohesiveness depends on a shared sense of mission and the unimpeded flow of information through the chain of command. African-Americans experienced discriminatory treatment in the military, even during integration, but the concerns and perceptions of African-American personnel were often unknown, unaddressed or both, in part because the lines of authority, from the military police to the officer corps, were almost exclusively white. . . . Indeed, "communication between the largely white officer corps and black enlisted men could be so tenuous that a commander might remain blissfully unaware of patterns of racial discrimination that black servicemen found infuriating."[3]

Making matters worse, many white officers had no idea how serious the problem was. "Violence and even death proved necessary to drive home the realization that the various assistant secretaries, special assistants, and even commanding officers had only the faintest idea what the black man and woman in the service were thinking." . . . Ultimately, "[t]he military of the 1970s recognized that its race problem was so critical that it was on the verge of self-destruction."[4]

This argument from the military was introduced by the justices of the Supreme Court themselves in oral arguments; it was clear then, as well as in the eventual decisions, that the insights of the retired military leaders had an impact on the justices. Justice Ruth Bader Ginsberg asked,

What is your answer to the argument made in that brief that there simply is no other way to have Armed Forces in which minorities will be represented not only largely among the enlisted members, but also among the officer cadre?[5]

This question from Justice Ginsburg found answer in the cogent majority decision she signed, which was authored by Justice Sandra Day O'Connor:

[H]igh-ranking retired officers and civilian leaders of the United States military assert that, "[b]ased on [their] decades of experience," a "highly qualified, racially diverse officer corps . . . is essential to the military's ability to fulfill its principle mission to provide national security." . . . At present, "the military cannot achieve an officer corps that is *both* highly qualified *and* racially diverse unless the service academies and the ROTC used limited race-conscious recruiting and admissions policies."[6]

Given the strong pronouncements of the Supreme Court regarding admissions policies, our universities can proceed with some certainty about the next steps we need to take in order to comply with the guidelines the Court issued. But our universities also must address issues that go far beyond our campuses, because we must work toward the goal that Justice O'Connor articulated:

> We expect that 25 years from now, the use of racial preferences will no longer be necessary to further the interest approved today.[7]

The Court suggests that universities study and emulate programs that are designed to provide diversity without the explicit policy of affirmative action, such as those programs created in states where affirmative action may not be applied in college admissions. But I would maintain that even with the implementation of beneficial new programs, we must address more elemental issues regarding the applicant pool of qualified students.

To put it simply, we are not educating enough minority students, and are not educating them well enough, to assure that minority applicants will comprise a significant percentage of our applicant pool within the next twenty-five years. We must begin to tackle this problem on several fronts.

First, we must find ways to improve the elementary and secondary school experiences of minority students. This will require effort from government, from school boards, from colleges and universities, and from families. We will need to work together to create better opportunities—a wider array of advanced courses and excellent teachers—to prepare children for the day that they apply to college. Many of the schools in our cities function in areas of poverty and have significant minority enrollments. These are the schools to which we need to bring ideas and resources, because we cannot afford to lose the minds and lives that could flourish with better opportunities. Justice Steven Breyer noted these problems in the discussion during the oral arguments of our cases:

> [W]e live in a world where more than half of all the minority—really 75 percent of black students below the college level—are at schools that are more than 50 percent minority. And 85 percent of those schools are in areas of poverty. . . . [M]any people feel in the schools, the universities, that the way—the only way to break this cycle is to have a leadership that is diverse. And to have a leadership across the country that is diverse, you have to train a diverse student body for law, for the military, for business, for all the other positions in this country that will allow us to have a diverse leadership in a country that is diverse.[8]

In addition to the actual circumstances of the schools, we must also work to overcome the achievement gap of minority students. Too often, self-imposed fears hold these students back, a cycle of misperception that needs to be broken. Research has revealed the complications that institutions and students face in overcoming stereotypical perceptions: "it is . . . difficult to design programs to overcome 'the threat in the air' that is the hallmark of stereotype vulnerability, for this involves a manipulation of students' deepest feelings, which are often unconscious or unacknowledged."[9]

When students see themselves as less qualified, they lack the confidence necessary to succeed in the competitive academic world. At the University of Michigan, we have been dedicated to the idea that every student we admit is qualified to be admitted, and the reason we argued so vigorously for the continuation of affirmative action was that we did not intend to lower our standards to create a broader pool of minority students. Once the students are on our campuses, we will need to make sure that they are entering a welcome environment that encourages all students to strive for success, and to eliminate the false perception of differential standards.

At every turn, we need to contradict the notion that diversity is incompatible with excellence; the two go hand in hand. Indeed, the Court recognized that diversity has educational benefits for all students and is therefore a matter of educational quality as well as equality. In doing so, the Court rejected Justice Scalia's suggestion that there is an inherent trade-off between diversity and quality:

> [T]he problem is a problem of Michigan's own creation, that is to say, it has decided to create an elite law school, it is one of the best law schools in the country. And there are few State law schools that—that get to that level. . . . Now, if Michigan really cares enough about that racial imbalance, why doesn't it do as many other State law schools do, lower the standards, not have a flagship elite law school, it solves the problem.[10]

We will need to bring not only our resources, but our research and ingenuity to these problems. We brought an impressive array of research to our defense at all levels of these lawsuits, as Professor Gurin has indicated in her essay in this volume, and now we must ask our experts not only to begin to study the new questions we face, but to help us define what those questions should be.

We are twenty-five years removed from the *Bakke* case, which helped establish a policy of affirmative action, but the Supreme Court's new decisions carry much more responsibility than did *Bakke*. Not only do we need to define our policies within the context of these newest decisions, but we also must utilize our new policies in a way that will allow us to end them. The Court has handed us a very complicated assignment, and a putative deadline. In the next twenty-five years, we must accomplish far more than we managed to do in the period from 1978 to 2003. But our society now has a deeper understanding of these complex issues, which has led to clear guidance from the Court, and a sound foundation on which to construct our critical next steps.

Notes

Acknowledgments

In addition to all of the remarkable people, many of whom are referenced in this volume, that brought their considerable intelligence to bear in defending this case, the lawyers, the administrators, the scholars, students, and alumni, and the friends across the country, I would like to thank the hearty members of the Office of the Provost and the Office of Undergraduate Admissions who toiled to mount this defense over so many years. Furthermore, I am indebted to Laura Calkins for her remarkable work in the Bentley Historical Library collections, and to Jo Thomas for her trenchant editorial comments.

1. Sandra Day O'Connor, writing for the majority in *Grutter v. Bollinger*, No. 02–241, Supreme Court, June 23, 2003, 3–4.

2. *Compelling Interest*, filed in *Gratz v. Bollinger*, No. 97–75321 in the U.S. District Court for the Eastern District of Michigan, and *Grutter v. Bollinger*, No. 97–75928 in the U.S. District Court for the Eastern District of Michigan, includes expert testimony by social scientists.

3. Otto Kerner, *Report of the National Advisory Commission on Civil Disorders* (Washington, D.C.: U.S. Government Printing Office, 1968), 1.

4. Expert report of Thomas J. Sugrue, *Gratz* and *Grutter*, District Court.

5. Expert report of Claude M. Steele, *Gratz* and *Grutter*, District Court.

6. Sugrue, expert report, 26–27.

7. See also the record of scholarship on the contact hypothesis summarized in the amicus briefs in *Gratz v. Bollinger* and *Grutter v. Bollinger*, Nos. 02–516 and 02–241 in the Supreme Court of the United States, filed by the American Educational Research Association, Association of American Colleges and Universities, American Association for Higher Education, and American Sociological Association. Expert report of Patricia Gurin, *Gratz* and *Gutter*, District Court.

8. *Arizona Republic*, April 18, 2003, B-10.

9. See Angelo N. Ancheta, *Revisiting "Bakke" and Diversity-Based Admissions: Constitutional Law, Social Science Research, and the University of Michigan Affirmative Action Cases,* Civil Rights Project at Harvard University, March 2003, http://www.civilrightsproject.harvard.edu/.

10. Thomas J. Kane, "Misconceptions in the Debate of Affirmative Action in College Admissions," in *Chilling Admissions: The Affirmative Action Crisis and the Search for Alternatives,* ed. Gary Orfield and Edward Miller (Cambridge: Civil Rights Project, Harvard University, 1998).

11. See Claude M. Steele, professor of psychology at Stanford University, and Patricia Gurin et al. in *Compelling Interest.*

12. Expert report of Patricia Gurin, *Gratz* and *Grutter,* District Court.

13. Peter Irons, *Jim Crow's Children: The Broken Promise of the Brown Decision* (New York: Viking Penguin, 2002), 199.

14. Ibid., 198–99.

15. Ibid., 199.

16. Amicus brief filed by the American Federation of Labor and the Congress of Industrial Organizations in *Gratz* and *Grutter,* Supreme Court, 17.

CHAPTER I

1. Gunnar Myrdal, *An American Dilemma: The Negro Problem and Modern Democracy,* 2 vols. (New York: Pantheon, 1972).

2. Myrdal, *An American Dilemma,* 1:lxix.

3. I develop this concept more extensively in "Race, Equity, and Democracy: African Americans and the Struggle over Civil Rights," in *The Social Construction of Democracy,* ed. George Reid Andrews and Herrick Chapman (New York: New York University Press, 1995), 193–217.

4. Dinesh D'Souza, *The End of Racism* (New York: Free Press, 1995).

5. Rayford Logan, *The Betrayal of the Negro: From Rutherford B. Hayes to Woodrow Wilson* (New York: Collier, 1965).

6. Numerous works treat the rise of Jim Crow and its consequences for blacks, whites, and others. For a sample read C. Vann Woodward, *The Strange Career of Jim Crow* (New York: Oxford University Press, 1974); Joel Williamson, *A Rage for Order: Black-White Relations in the American South since Emancipation* (New York: Oxford University Press, 1986); and Glenda Gilmore, *Gender and Jim Crow: Women and the Politics of White Supremacy in North Carolina, 1896–1920* (Chapel Hill: University of North Carolina Press, 1996).

7. For a delineation of the various organizations and campaigns see Robin D. G. Kelley and Earl Lewis, eds., *To Make Our World Anew: A History of African Americans* (New York: Oxford University Press, 2000), especially chaps. 5 and 6, by Noralee Frankel and Barbara Bair, respectively. Earlier discussion of the myriad new organizations that came of age after the Civil War is presented in John Hope Franklin, *From Slavery to Freedom*, 5th ed. (New York: Alfred A. Knopf, 1980), 268–94, 318–22, 349–82. A few of those institutions were schools of higher education. Read James D. Anderson, *The Education of Blacks in the South, 1860–1935* (Chapel Hill: University of North Carolina Press, 1988), chap. 7.

8. For a portrait of blacks in New Orleans and the social relations born of slavery see John Blassingame, *Black New Orleans* (Chicago: University of Chicago Press, 1973).

9. As quoted in Richard Kluger, *Simple Justice* (New York: Vintage, 1977), 72. See also Edward L. Ayers, *The Promise of the New South: Life after Reconstruction* (New York: Oxford University Press, 1992), chap. 6; and Charles F. Lofgren, *The Plessy Case: A Legal-Historical Interpretation* (New York: Oxford University Press, 1987).

10. *Plessy v. Ferguson*, 163 U.S. 537; 16 S. Ct. 1138; 41 L. Ed. 256 (1896).

11. Richard Sears, *A Utopian Experiment in Kentucky: Integration and Social Equality at Berea, 1866–1904* (Westport, Conn.: Greenwood Press, 1996), details the history of interracial relations as well as the consequences of the court's verdict.

12. Kluger, *Simple Justice*, 87.

13. The treatment of blacks at one university is explored in Werner Sollors, Caldwell Titcomb, and Thomas A. Underwood, eds., *Blacks at Harvard: A Documentary History of African-American Experience at Harvard and Radcliffe* (New York: New York University Press, 1993). See also Genna Rae McNeil, *Groundwork: Charles Hamilton Houston and the Struggle for Civil Rights* (Philadelphia: University of Pennsylvania Press, 1983); and Juan Williams, *Thurgood Marshall: American Revolutionary* (New York: Times Books, 1998), 15–100.

14. Williams, *Thurgood Marshall*, 52–100.

15. Kluger, *Simple Justice*, 188; Carl T. Rowan, *Dream Makers, Dream Breakers* (Boston: Little, Brown, 1993), 50–57.

16. *Missouri ex. rel Gaines v. Canada* (1938) 59 S. Ct. 232, 305 U.S. 337, 83 L. Ed. 208; Kluger, *Simple Justice*, 212. Years later Marshall bristled when he recalled both the astounding victory and the fact that Gaines had simply disappeared by 1940, no doubt tired of the appeals and the spotlight. As a result

he never attended the university. See Rowan, *Dream Makers, Dream Keepers*, 77–78.

17. For a summary of the literary texts see Nathan Irvin Huggins, *Harlem Renaissance* (New York: Oxford University Press, 1971). An overview of texts spanning the twentieth century can be found in David Roediger, ed., *Black on White: Black Writers on What It Means to Be White* (New York: Schocken, 1998). No Harlem Renaissance writer wrote so poignantly about the mutability of race as Nella Larson in the novels *Quicksand* (1928) and *Passing* (1929). The literature on whiteness has grown exponentially in the last decade. A sample includes David Roediger, *Wages of Whiteness: Race and the Making of the American Working Class* (London: Verso, 1991); Toni Morrison, *Playing in the Dark: Whiteness and the Literary Imagination* (Cambridge: Harvard University Press, 1992); Noel Ignatiev, *How the Irish Became White* (New York: Routledge, 1995); Grace Elizabeth Hale, *Making Whiteness: The Culture of Segregation in the South, 1890–1940* (New York: Pantheon, 1998); Matthew Frye Jacobson, *Whiteness of a Different Color* (Cambridge: Harvard University Press, 1998); and Thomas Guglielmo, *White on Arrival: Italians, Race, Color, and Power in Chicago, 1890–1945* (New York: Oxford University Press, 2003).

18. Ronald Takaki, *Strangers from a Different Shore: A History of Asian Americans* (Boston: Little, Brown, 1989), chap. 10.

19. Kelley and Lewis, *Make the World Anew*, 435–44.

20. Kluger, *Simple Justice*, 258–60.

21. Charles M. Payne. *I've Got the Light of Freedom: The Organizing Tradition and the Mississippi Freedom Struggle* (Berkeley: University of California Press, 1995), 1–66; John Dittmer, *Local People: The Struggle for Civil Rights in Mississippi* (Urbana: University of Illinois Press), 1–115.

22. *McLaurin v. Oklahoma State Regents*, 339 U.S. 637; 70 S. Ct. 851; 96 L. Ed. 1149 (1950). *Sweatt v. Painter*, 339 U.S. 629; 70 S. Ct. 848; 94 L. Ed. 1114 (1950). Kluger, *Simple Justice*, 260–88.

23. One child's memories of the difficulties of desegregation are captured in Melba Beals, *Warriors Don't Cry* (New York: Pocket Books, 1994). Details of the period can be found in Kelley and Lewis, *Make the World Anew*, 473–78. See also Numan Bartley, *The New South, 1945–1980* (Baton Rouge: Louisiana State University Press, 1995), chaps. 5–8; Benjamin Muse, *Virginia's Massive Resistance* (Bloomington: Indiana University Press, 1961). As L. Douglas Smith notes in *Managing White Supremacy* (Chapel Hill: University of North Carolina Press, 2002), *Brown* signaled the end of whites' ability to dominate the shaping of racial relations in the Old Dominion. This hastened the path to massive resistance. For the aftermath of desegregation in one southern city read Robert A. Pratt, *The*

Color of Their Skin: Education and Race in Richmond, Virginia, 1954–89 (Charlottesville: University Press of Virginia, 1992). For a systematic examination of the resegregation of public schools see Erika Frankenberg and Chungmei Lee, "Race in American Public Schools: Rapidly Resegregating School Districts," August 8, 2002, Civil Rights Project, Harvard University, http://www.civilrights project.harvard.edu/research/deseg/ reseg_schools02 .php.

24. The positions of various organizations contributing to anti–affirmative action efforts are prominently advertised on Web sites and other documents. See American Civil Rights Institute, www.acri.org, a not-for-profit organization founded by Ward Connerly "aimed at educating the public about the need to move beyond racial and gender preferences"; the American Enterprise Institute at www.aei.org; the Ashbrook Center, a vigorous opponent of affirmative action, at Ashland University, www.ashbrook.org; the Center for Equal Opportunity bills itself as the "only think tank devoted exclusively to the promotion of colorblind equal opportunity and racial harmony" (www.ceousa.org). The group also includes the Center for Individual Rights, which filed suit against the University of Michigan on behalf of the named plaintiffs (www.cir-usa.org); Citizens' Initiative on Race and Ethnicity (CIRE; www.cire.org) acknowledges there have been difficult times in the racial past but champions a forward-looking view that looks optimistically at a world where we have moved beyond race. Others active in the social movement to oppose affirmative action include Claremont Institute for the Study of Statesmanship and the Political Philosophy, www.claremont.org; Council for International Security Ethics and Public Policy Center (www.Claremont.org), which seeks to "clarify and reinforce the bond between the Judeo-Christian moral tradition and the public debate over domestic and foreign policy issues"; the Federalist Society, a network of conservatives and libertarians, which strongly supports "individual liberty" and "traditional values" (www.fed-soc.org); the Heritage Foundation (www.heritage.org); and the Independent Women's Forum (www.iwf.org), which opposes the categorizing of Americans.

As William Rusher notes, the demarcation between the old Right and the New Right is imperfect at best. Concerns over communism, liberalism, and civil rights galvanized and energized a reformulation of coalitions, ultimately producing an end to the Democratic Party's control of the South by the 1970s. Rusher, *The Rise of the Right* (New York: William Morrow, 1984); Earl Black and Merle Black, *The Rise of Southern Republicans* (Cambridge: Harvard University Press, 2002).

25. Carol M. Swain, "Affirmative Action: Legislative History, Judicial Interpretations, Public Consensus," in *America Becoming: Racial Trends and*

Their Consequences, ed. Neil J. Smelser, William Julius Wilson, and Faith Mitchell (Washington, D.C.: National Academy Press, 2001), 1:319–22.

26. Borgna Brunner, "Timeline of Affirmative Action Milestones," http://www.infoplease.com/spot/affirmativetimeline1.html.

27. John David Skrentny, *Ironies of Affirmative Action* (Chicago: University of Chicago Press, 1996), 193–211.

28. Swain, "Affirmative Action," 320; Thomas Sowell, *A Conflict of Visions* (New York: William Morrow, 1987).

29. Black and Black, *Rise of Southern Republicans,* 148–73.

30. On housing segregation see Douglas S. Massey and Nancy A. Denton, *American Apartheid: Segregation and the Making of the Underclass* (Cambridge: Harvard University Press, 1993), especially 1–114. The volatility of busing is explored in Ronald A. Formisano, *Boston against Busing: Race, Class, and Ethnicity in the 1960s and 1970s* (Chapel Hill: University of North Carolina Press, 1993).

31. As quoted in Robert A. Pratt, *We Shall Not Be Moved: The Desegregation of the University of Georgia* (Athens: University of Georgia Press, 2002), 155.

32. *Regents of the University of California v. Bakke,* 438 U.S. 265 (1978); Joel Dreyfuss and Charles Lawrence III, *The Bakke Case: The Politics of Inequality* (New York: Harcourt Brace Jovanovich, 1979); and Wayne McCormack, ed., *The Bakke Decision: Implications for Higher Education Admissions,* A Report of the ACE-AALS Committee on Bakke (Washington, D.C.: American Council on Education and Association of American Law Schools, 1978).

33. Philip S. Foner, ed., *The Voice of Black America,* vol. 2 (New York: Capricorn Books, 1972), 428.

34. Reynolds Farley and Walter Allen, *The Color Line and the Quality of Life in America* (New York: Oxford University Press, 1989), 209–98.

35. Farley and Allen, *The Color Line,* chap. 11; Gerald David Jaynes and Robin M. Williams, eds., *A Common Destiny: Blacks and American Society* (Washington, D.C.: National Academy Press, 1989), 294–328. As Andrew Hacker, in *Two Nations: Black and White, Separate, Hostile, and Unequal* (New York: Charles Scribner's Sons, 1992), 93–133, and Melvin Oliver and Thomas M. Shapiro, in *Black Wealth, White Wealth: A New Perspective on Racial Inequality* (New York: Routledge, 1995), note, a racial income gap still persists, as does a more pronounced wealth gap.

36. See note 35.

37. Jaynes and Williams, *A Common Destiny,* 17–18, 23–25, 526–48.

38. See Lewis, "Race, Equity, and Democracy," 203–13.

39. Skrentny, *Ironies of Affirmative Action,* 37. Almost all of the states extended the same preferences to veterans, modeled after the Veterans Preference Act of 1944.

40. Nicholas Lemann, public lecture, America Values Series, University of Michigan, April 1998, and *The Big Test: The Secret History of the American Meritocracy* (New York: Farrar, Straus and Giroux, 1999).

41. Richard J. Herrnstein and Charles Murray, *The Bell Curve: Intelligence and Class Structure in American Life* (New York: Free Press, 1994), for example.

42. A sample of the press coverage in the first year, 1997: Jonathan Chait, "U-M Admissions," *Detroit Free Press,* December 9; "The Diversity Myth," editorial, *Detroit News,* December 7; Rene Sanchez, "Final Exam for Campus Affirmative Action?" *Washington Post,* December 5; Pat Griffith, "College Defends Racial Quotas," *Pittsburgh Post-Gazette,* December 4; John A. Woods, "U-M Prepared for Cost of Defending Policy," *Ann Arbor News,* December 4; Clarence Page, "Preferences Fight Sends Wrong Message," *Detroit News,* December 2; *Ann Arbor News* staff, "Affirmative Action to Be Forum Focus," *Ann Arbor News,* November 16; Maryanne George, "U-M Turns Hot Topic into Series of Lectures," *Detroit Free Press,* November 14; John A. Woods, "U-M Suit May Add One or More Plaintiffs," *Ann Arbor News,* November 14; Larry R. Kostecke, "Lawsuit Attacks UM's Weird Politics of Privilege," *Flint Journal,* November 10; Adam Cohen, "The Next Great Battle over Affirmative Action," *Time,* November 10; John A. Woods, "Assembly Backs Diversity," *Ann Arbor News,* November 5; "Race Policy," editorial, *Ann Arbor News,* November 4; *Ann Arbor News* staff, "U-M: Admissions Lawsuit Unaffected by Court Ruling," *Ann Arbor News,* November 4; Maryanne George, "Students Decry Suit Attacking U-M Policy," *Detroit Free Press,* October 31; Peggy Walsh-Sarnecki, "If It Loses Suit, U-M Could See Fewer Minorities," *Detroit Free Press,* October 31; Peggy Walsh-Sarnecki, "Affirmative Action Lawsuits Similar in Texas, Michigan," *Detroit Free Press,* October 31; Maryanne George, "Minority Enrollment Stays Constant for U-M, MSU," *Detroit Free Press,* October 29; John A. Woods, "Bollinger Warns of Lawsuit's Impact," *Ann Arbor News,* October 28; "The Politics of Preferences," editorial, *Detroit News,* October 1; Todd Dvorak, "Anti–affirmative Action Forum Disrupted," *Ann Arbor News,* September 30; Peggy Walsh-Sarnecki, "Clash of Affirmative Action," *Detroit Free Press,* September 30; Peggy Walsh-Sarnecki and Maryanne George, "Jaye Presses Quotas Debate: He Looks for Backing in Suit Targeting U-M," *Detroit Free*

Press, September 27; "U-M Admissions: School Rightly Strives to Keep Diversity in Its Policy," editorial, *Detroit Free Press,* September 27; "U-M: Race Counts," editorial, *Detroit News,* July 24; Sharon Terlep, "U-M's Admissions Policies under Attack: Plan to Do Away with Records on Race Poses New Questions to Probe," *State News,* July 24; Peggy Walsh-Sarnecki, "U-M Criticized for Giving Some Applicants Advantage," *Detroit Free Press,* July 18; Fiona Rose, "Universities Need Students Who Offer More Than Grades," *Detroit Free Press,* July 17; Rusty Hoover, "U-M List Gives Preference to Privileged, Critics Charge: University Says It Adjusts Grades of Applicants Based on Quality of High School Only as a Guideline," *Detroit News,* July 17; Susan L. Oppat, "U-M System Favors Certain High Schools," *Ann Arbor News,* July 17; Rusty Hoover and Jenny Nolan, "Do Celebrities Make the U-M Grade?" *Detroit News,* July 17; "Affirmative Action," editorial, *Detroit Free Press,* July 16; Peter Luke, "Not Enough Gains Yet to Give Up on Affirmative Action," *Ann Arbor News,* July 1; *Grand Haven Tribune* staff, "U-M Discrimination," *Grand Haven Tribune,* June 24; Dave Jaye, "Judge Them on Achievement," *Sturgis Journal,* June 24; *Ann Arbor News* staff, "U-M May Face Suit over Race Based Admissions," *Ann Arbor News,* June 23; *Herald-Palladium* staff, "Some Claim U-M's Admissions Policies Unfair to Whites," *Herald-Palladium,* June 23; Rusty Hoover, "U-M Employs Points System to Determine Admissions," *Detroit News,* June 22.

43. Henry Vance Davis, ed., "Sankofa: The University since BAM: Twenty Years of Progress?" conference report, University of Michigan, Office of Minority Affairs, ca. 1990; *Harper's Weekly* quote in Howard H. Peckham, *The Making of the University of Michigan,* ed. Margaret L. Steneck and Nicholas Steneck (Ann Arbor: Bentley Historical Library, 1994), 95. President James Angell underscored this point in his 1879 commencement address: "The Higher Education: A Plea for Making It Accessible to All," June 25, 1879. Angell Presidental Papers, Bentley Library.

44. Peckham, *Making of University,* 64, 67, 189–90, 278, 294–95, 312–13.

45. Peckham, *Making of University,* 310–16, 346–54.

46. This point is fully delineated in the intervenors' case before the courts: "U-M Response to Intervenors' Petition for Writ of Certiorari in *Gratz,*" http://www.umich.edu/~urel/admissions/legal/gratz/gra-iopcert.html.

47. Affirmative Action Review, Report to the President, July 6, 1995, sec. 2, http://clinton1.nara.gov/White_House/EOP/OP/html/aa/aa02.html.

48. The long-term consequences of educating a racially and ethnically diverse population at the nation's most selective institutions are explicated with care in William G. Bowen and Derek Bok, *The Shape of the River: Long-*

Term Consequences of Considering Race in College and University Admissions (Princeton: Princeton University Press, 1998).

CHAPTER 2

President of Cornell University. I appreciate comments I received on an earlier draft from Evan Caminker and Kathy Okun.

1. In an early era, some resisted the term *integration,* insisting that they were committed only to a more limited ideal of *desegregation.* I found it striking that no one invoked this distinction to me during the litigation; my sense is that this distinction has lost salience and today there is little public resistance to the ideal of integration.

2. Elements of the *Grutter* opinion could be read as suggesting that the state may have a sufficiently compelling interest in the integration of other institutions in society (such as the military) that it may take affirmative steps to achieve that goal. In the case of universities, the institutional interest involved their status as the critical path to leadership and success in America; other situations may require the identification of other interests of comparable significance.

3. To be clear, I do not mean to imply that Justice Powell himself did not appreciate the connection between integration and democratic legitimacy. I am suggesting only that, because such an appreciation did not manifest itself in the *Bakke* opinion, universities felt constrained to speak about affirmative action in ways that feel less authentic than the ways they may speak about the subject after *Grutter.*

CHAPTER 3

1. "The Compelling Need for Diversity in Higher Education, Expert Reports Prepared for *Gratz v. Bollinger et al.,* 122 F.Supp.2d 811 (E.D.Mich. 2000) (No. 97–75231) and *Grutter v. Bollinger et al.,* 137 F.Supp.2d 821 (E.D. Mich. 2001) (No. 97–75928)," available at http://www.umich.edu/~urel/ admissions/research/expert. This document also includes expert testimony by other social scientists: Thomas Sugrue, then associate professor of history and sociology at the University of Pennsylvania; Eric Foner, DeWitt Clinton Professor of History at Columbia University; Albert M. Camarillo, professor of history and director of the Center for Comparative Studies of Race and Eth-

nicity at Stanford University; William G. Bowen, president of the Andrew W. Mellon Foundation and previously president of Princeton University; Claude M. Steele, professor of psychology at Stanford University; and Derek Bok, the Three Hundredth Anniversary University Professor at the John F. Kennedy School of Government at Harvard University and previously president of Harvard University.

2. The expert testimony was based on the collaboration of all of the authors of this chapter, although only one of us (Patricia Gurin) was formally the expert witness.

3. These features of an environment that promote mental activity are compatible with the cognitive-developmental theories we described earlier. In general, those theories suggest that cognitive growth is fostered by *novelty, instability, discontinuity,* and *discrepancy.* To grow cognitively, we need to be in situations that lead to a state of uncertainty, and even possibly anxiety (Piaget, 1971, 1985; Ruble 1994; Acredolo and O'Connor 1991; Berlyne 1970; Doise and Palmonari 1984).

4. In all analyses we also control for personal background characteristics of the students (gender, SAT composite of verbal and math scores, high school grade point average, ethnic diversity of the high school and of the precollege neighborhood), and in the case of the national study for characteristics of institutions (percentage of undergraduates at the student's college who are not white, selectivity as indicated by the mean SAT composite score of the entering freshman class, university versus four-year college, private versus public status, institutional diversity emphasis as indicated by students perceptions at each college about the degree to which the institution emphasizes diversity as an institutional goal, and faculty diversity emphasis as indicated by student perceptions at each college concerning the degree to which faculty incorporate diversity issues into the curriculum).

5. The classroom diversity measure in the MSS involves more than just exposure to content about racial and ethnic groups. Students' answers to these classroom questions likely referred to classes that exposed them to racially/ethnically diverse students as well as to curriculum content. In 1994, when these students were seniors, they had to have taken at least one course that met the Race and Ethnicity Requirement. To meet that requirement, the Literature, Sciences, and Arts College had approved 111 courses. We obtained the racial/ethnic distribution of students in those courses for 1993–94, the year that the MSS gathered senior data. Two-thirds of these courses had enrolled between 20 and 80 percent students of color.

6. Findings on Latino/a students were presented only for the national

study. The number of Latino/a students in the Michigan Student Study was too small for our multiple regression analyses.

7. Rothman, Lipset, and Nevitte (2003) claim that most of the positive evidence of diversity has come from studies asking students to assess its impact themselves. This is a false claim in that the vast majority of research is of the type that ties diversity experiences statistically to measures of student outcomes that do not even mention diversity.

8. As noted above, findings on Latino/a students were presented only for the national study.

9. Of course, some students of color were randomly assigned room-mates of color as well. The *N* of these pairings was too small, however, to analyze the effects of this pairing versus a randomly assigned white roommate from the perspectives of the students of color.

10. We do not indicate here questions about narrowly methodological aspects of our research such as questions about the survey samples, the size of effects, the adequacy of some of our measures. Answers to those questions appear in our responses on Michigan's website.

11. Fewer than twenty amicus briefs were submitted on behalf of the plaintiffs. The number and breadth of American society represented by those briefs were much less impressive than were those briefs submitted in behalf of the University of Michigan.

AFTERWORD

1. Brief for General Motors Corporation as Amicus Curiae 2.

2. Brief for Music Television Networks as Amicus Curiae 9.

3. Brief for Julius W. Becton, Jr. et al. as Amici Curiae 14.

4. Brief for Julius W. Becton, Jr. et al. as Amici Curiae 16.

5. Justice Ruth Bader Ginsburg, question during the oral arguments for *Grutter v. Bollinger,* April 1, 2003; http://www.supremecourtus.gov/oral_arguments/argument_transcripts/02-241.pdf, 7.

6. *Grutter v. Bollinger,* 18–19.

7. *Grutter v. Bollinger,* 31.

8. Justice Stephen G. Breyer, question during the oral arguments for *Grutter v. Bollinger,* April 1, 2003; http://www.supremecourtus.gov/oral_arguments/argument_transcripts/02-241.pdf, 13.

9. Douglas S. Massey, Camille Z. Charles, Garvey F. Lundy, and Mary J. Fischer, *The Source of the River: The Social Origins of Freshmen at America's*

Selective Colleges and Universities (Princeton, N.J.: Princeton University Press, 2003), 195.

10. Justice Antonin Scalia, question during the oral arguments for *Grutter v. Bollinger,* April 1, 2003; http://www.supremecourtus.gov/oral_arguments/argument_transcripts/02–241.pdf, 30–31.

Contributors

Nancy Cantor is Chancellor of the University of Illinois at Urbana-Champaign. She was Provost and Executive Vice President for Academic Affairs at the University of Michigan when the affirmative action lawsuits were filed and was deeply involved in organizing the social science defense in those cases. At Michigan she has also been Dean of the Horace H. Rackham School of Graduate Studies and Vice Provost for Academic Affairs. She is a former Chair of the Department of Psychology at Princeton University. She received her A.B. in 1974 from Sarah Lawrence College and her Ph.D. in psychology in 1978 from Stanford University. Dr. Cantor is a fellow of the American Academy of Arts and Sciences and a member of the Institute of Medicine of the National Academy of Sciences.

Mary Sue Coleman is the President of the University of Michigan and also holds appointments as Professor of Biological Chemistry in the Medical School and Professor of Chemistry in the College of Literature, Science, and the Arts. President Coleman was the chief spokesperson for the university during the phases of the lawsuits that took place at the United States Supreme Court, working closely with Vice President and General Counsel Marvin Krislov to craft the defense and response of the university during the oral arguments and final decisions. Dr. Coleman then presided over the development of a new undergraduate admissions process at the University of Michigan, in compliance with the rulings of the Court. President Coleman received her undergraduate degree in chemistry from Grinnell College, and her Ph.D. in biochemistry from the University of North Carolina. She is the former Provost of the University of New Mexico and served as President of the University of Iowa for seven years. Elected to the Institute of Medicine of the National Academy of Sciences in 1997, she is also a Fellow of the American Association for the Advancement of Science and of the American Academy of Arts and Sciences.

Eric L. Dey is Executive Associate Dean and Associate Dean for Research for the University of Michigan School of Education and Associate Professor in the Center for the Study of Higher and Post-secondary Education. Professor Dey was one of the chief architects of the social science research produced in Patricia Gurin's expert witness report that supported the University of Michigan's legal position on the use of affirmative action in college admissions. Dey's research is concerned with the ways that colleges and universities shape the experiences and lives of students and faculty. The central concern of this work is identifying the influences that different institutional structures have on individuals and the degree to which these influences are dependent on the evolving context within which the enterprise of higher education operates.

Gerald Gurin is a Professor and Research Scientist Emeritus at the University of Michigan in Ann Arbor. Since his retirement, he has continued to conduct research with the university's Office of Academic Multicultural Initiatives (OAMI). A major focus of his research and teaching is the impact of higher education on students and the increasing inclusion of racial/ethnic minorities in higher education. His publications include *Inner-City Negro Youth in a Job Training Project: A Study of Factors Related to Attrition and Job Success* (1968) and *Americans View Their Mental Health* (1957).

Patricia Gurin is Nancy Cantor Distinguished University Professor, Emerita, of Psychology and Women's Studies at the University of Michigan. During her tenure at the University of Michigan she chaired the Department of Psychology and served as Interim Dean of the College of Literature, Science, and the Arts. One of the founders of the Program on Intergroup Relations, a nationally recognized program that uses intergroup dialogues to foster cultural competence among students, she is now directing its research program. She was an expert witness in the affirmative action cases that were decided by the Supreme Court in 2003. A social psychologist, she works on social identity and its relationship to intergroup relations and political participation. She is the author or editor of numerous books, chapters in edited volumes, and articles, including the books *Black Consciousness, Identity, and Achievement; Hope and Independence: Blacks' Responses to Electoral and Party Politics;* and *Women, Politics, and Change.*

Sylvia Hurtado is Professor of Education at the University of California at Los Angeles and Director of the Higher Education Research Institute. She was the Director of the Center for the Study of Higher Education and Associate Professor at the University of Michigan during the years of the affirmative action cases and was a member of the research team that assisted with the multicampus study of college students as part of the expert witness report of Patricia Gurin. Her research extends the social science research evidence presented in the cases, focusing on the cognitive, social, and democratic skills of undergraduates and how universities prepare students to participate in a diverse democracy.

Jeffrey S. Lehman is the President of Cornell University. He was a member of the University of Michigan Law School faculty from 1987 to 2003, and during the 1991–92 academic year he served on the committee that drafted the Law School admissions policy at issue in the Grutter litigation. From 1994 to 2003, he was Dean of the Law School. In that capacity, he was responsible for implementing the admissions policy and for representing the Law School to the public during the litigation. He was also a member of the team that developed and implemented the university's overall litigation strategy.

Earl Lewis is Vice Provost and Dean of the Horace H. Rackham School of Graduate Studies at the University of Michigan and the Elsa Barkley Brown and Robin D. G. Kelley Collegiate Professor of History and African American and African Studies. A historian and the author or editor of six books and numerous essays and articles, he has emerged as a leading figure in graduate education in the United States and a vocal proponent of diversifying graduate schools. During the legal battles he served as one of several university spokespeople and organized the university's dialogues on diversity efforts.

Index

3M